Chuck and Blanche Johnson's Savor Cookbook®

Savor
Montana II
Cookbook

More of Montana's Finest Restaurants
Their Recipes and Their Histories

Wilderness Adventures Press, Inc.
Belgrade, Montana

Published by Wilderness Adventures Press, Inc.™
45 Buckskin Road
Belgrade, MT 59714
1-866-400-2012
Web site: www.wildadvpress.com
E-mail: books@wildadvpress.com

First Edition 2008

Chuck and Blanche Johnson's Savor Cookbook® Series

Printed in Malaysia

ISBN 978-1-932098-25-9

TABLE OF CONTENTS

Table of Contents

T.C. Power Store, Fort Benton, Montana. ca. 1870's

INTRODUCTION

This second edition of our popular *Savor Montana Cookbook* highlights many new restaurants and close to 100 new recipes, along with new historical photographs from the Montana Historical Society in Helena, Montana.

As with our entire Savor Cookbook Series™, all of the featured restaurants were by invitation. None of the restaurants are charged for appearing in the book. We selected them based on the excellence and uniqueness of their food, as well as their ambience. Many have interesting histories.

We are also happy to see more Montana restaurants including organic and local meats and produce on their menus. Montana has many ranchers and farmers that are focusing on sustainable foods. There was a reason that Nelson Story led one of the first cattle drives from Texas to Montana in the mid-19th century. Montana has long been known to grow high-protein grasses that are very beneficial for animal growth, first supporting the free-ranging bison and then the cattle and sheep that followed. Today, the emphasis on natural grass-fed also extends to pork. You will find several websites listed in our Culinary Sources appendix where you can purchase these wonderful meats, along with free-range chickens and turkeys.

The reader can use this book in several ways. As a travel guide, the reader can learn something about a restaurant's history, culinary philosophy, and ambience, as well as the type of cuisine that it features. The map in the front gives the reader a perspective of the state, and approximately where each restaurant is located.

Reading the recipes is an enjoyable way to get a "taste" of each restaurant, and trying them out at home can be fun for the home chef as well as for his or her guests. We hope you enjoy *Savor Montana Cookbook – II* as much as we have enjoyed putting it together.

Blanche and Chuck Johnson

Savor Montana II Cookbook

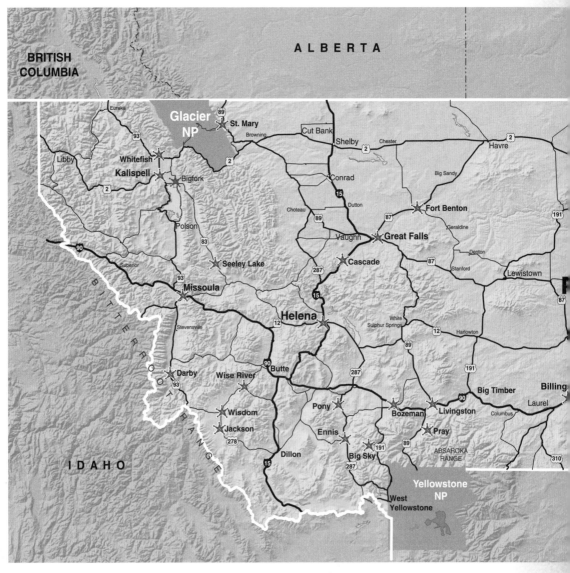

0   100 Miles

0   100KM

RESTAURANT LOCATIONS

FEATURED RESTAURANTS

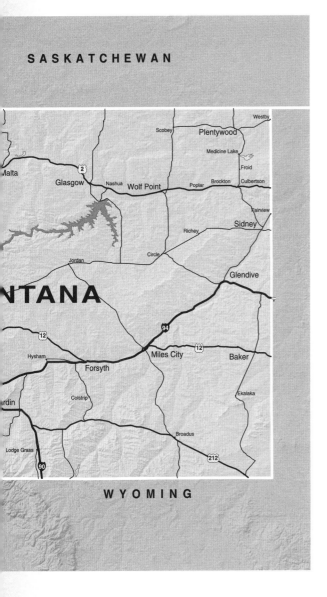

BIG SKY
320 Ranch
Buck's T-4
Lone Mountain Ranch
The Timbers at Moonlight Basin
BIGFORK
La Provence
BILLINGS
Enzo Mediterranean Grill
Q Cuisine
The Granary
Walkers Grill
BOZEMAN
Boodles
Ferraro's Fine Italian Restaurant
Gallatin River Lodge
John Bozeman's Bistro
CASCADE
The Flyfishers Inn
DARBY
Triple Creek Ranch
ENNIS
Continental Divide
FORT BENTON
Grand Union Hotel, Union Grille
GREAT FALLS
Ristorante Portofino
HELENA
The River Grille
JACKSON
Jackson Hot Springs Lodge
KALISPELL
Cafe Max
Painted Horse Grill
LIVINGSTON
Adagio
Second Street Bistro
MISSOULA
Red Bird
PONY
Potosi Hot Springs
PRAY
Chico Hot Springs
SEELEY LAKE
Double Arrow Resort
ST. MARY
Snowgoose Grille
WHITEFISH
Corner House Grille
Pollo Grill Rotisserie
Tupelo Grille
WISDOM
Big Hole Crossing
WISE RIVER
Big Hole Lodge

MONTANA FACTS

Fourth largest state in the union
    147,138 square miles
    93,157,953 acres
    550 miles east to west
    275 miles north to south
Elevations – 1,820 feet to 12,798 feet
Counties – 56
Towns and Cities – 126
Population (2000 census) – 902,195

7 Indian Reservations
2 National Parks
11 National Forests
68 State Recreation Areas
12 Wilderness Areas
11 State Parks
Nicknames
Treasure State
Big Sky Country
Land of the Shining Mountains

Interior of line. Lo Bull Camp between Pumpkin Creek and Mizpah. Slim Ridge shown inside cabin. ca. 1910

Primary Industries
    Agriculture
    Timber
    Mining
    Tourism
Capital – Helena
Bird – Western Meadowlark
Animal – Grizzly Bear
Flower – Bitterroot
Fish – Black-spotted Cutthroat
Tree – Ponderosa Pine
Gemstone – Montana Agate
Grass – Bluebunch Wheatgrass

Treaty Commission, 1879.

Enzo
Mediterranean
Bistro

Established 1998

1502 Rehberg Lane
Billings, MT 59102
406-651-0999

Reservations recommended
Lunch 11:30 am to 2:00 pm
(Tuesday thru Friday)
Dinner nightly at 5:00 pm

Enzo Mediterranean Bistro

James Honaker, Owner
Laurent Zirotti, General Manager

Over time, on its way to the Missouri, the Yellowstone River cut deep into the earth, creating the present-day Yellowstone Valley. This action exposed the magnificent sandstone cliffs that are today a Billings landmark. From the valley floor near the river, it's over 460 feet to the top of the rimrocks. Buffalo and other wildlife flourished along this broad valley and the adjacent plains during the early 19th century and served as a lifeline for Native Americans.

Even before Montana became a state in November of 1889, Billings was starting to prosper. The Minnesota and Montana Land and Improvement Company purchased Northern Pacific grant lands in the Billings area in 1882, which included land for forty miles on either side of the railroad tracks in that area. Up until that time, there were only three buildings on the site now known as Billings—a large wooden structure on Montana Avenue, which housed railroad engineers and supervisors, a store on Minnesota Avenue and a home on 27th Street. By the fall of that same year, 155 businesses, 99 homes, 6 railroad buildings, and a church were kicking off Billings's boom.

Today, Billings is the largest city in Montana and functions as the hub for a region larger than 125,000 square miles, and it remains a highly productive agricultural region for crops and cattle.

The Enzo Mediterranean Bistro is a relatively recent addition to the Billings culinary scene, but it has quickly gained a reputation as one of the best restaurants in the region.

It is a new building influenced by the Tuscan/Provence farmhouse architectural style. The varied menu includes a taste of the Mediterranean in addition to classic American dishes that include Montana's fine beef along with fresh fish arriving from both coasts. There is a fine selection of wines and beers to complement your meal.

General Manager Laurent Zirotti grew up in France. After meeting James Honaker in San Francisco, Laurent and his family moved to the Billings area to open and manage Enzo.

MUSSELS MARINIÈRE
Appetizer

Ingredients

5 pounds mussels (Penn Cove in USA)
1 ounce unsweetened butter
1 cup dry white wine
6 each shallots
Salt and pepper

2 ounces butter
1 ounce fresh parsley
OPTIONAL INGREDIENTS
Artichoke hearts, cooked
Roma tomatoes, diced

Preparation

WASH the mussels thoroughly.

IN A saucepan, combine mussels, unsweetened butter, white wine, diced shallots, salt, pepper, and half the chopped parsley (add artichokes and tomatoes at this point if you want). Cook over medium heat with a lid. Mussels are cooked when they open up. Do not serve mussels that do not open (discard). Put mussels in a serving dish and reduce the sauce to one-third. When sauce is ready, stop the fire and add the butter to the sauce with a whip (whisk). Add parsley to taste for seasoning and pour over mussels.

SPRINKLE the other half of parsley over dish.

Serves 8

Sautéed Stuffed Salmon
with Smoked Salmon—served with Citrus Salsa

For the Salmon

4 thick pieces of filet fresh salmon
4 thin slices of smoked salmon
   Basil pesto

Panko bread crumbs, preferably
Oil and butter

Preparation

BUTTERFLY each filet of fresh salmon (skin off). Spread filet with a tablespoon of basil pesto and lay a piece of smoked salmon in between, then fold back together. Bread lightly and sauté in a pan with butter and oil. Cook the salmon until brown on both sides and finish in oven until pink in the middle.

For the Citrus Salsa

1 orange cut into segments
2 tomatoes, diced
2 scallions, diced
1 garlic clove, chopped finely
5 leaves of basil, chopped

½ Bermuda onion, chopped finely
2 tablespoons of rice wine vinegar
3 tablespoons of olive oil
   Salt and pepper to taste

Preparation

COMBINE all prepared fruits and vegetables together, add vinegar, and while stirring, slowly add the olive oil.

SERVE cooked salmon over steamed rice and spoon Citrus Salsa on top.

Serves 4

Frozen Italian Bittersweet Chocolate Gelato

Ingredients

9 ounces bittersweet chocolate
  (best quality available)
⅔ cup heavy cream brought to a boil
7 egg yolks

1⅛ cups sugar (10 ounces)
2 cups heavy cream, whipped
2 ounces liqueur of your choice,
  such as Amaretto or Frangelica

Preparation

CHOP chocolate and melt over water bath. Whip yolks and sugar to ribbon stage. Add melted chocolate to ribboned yolks, then mix in hot cream. Add liqueur. Fold in whipped cream. Freeze in container and scoop, or freeze in individual molds.

TOP with an espresso whipped cream, powdered sugar, and powdered cocoa or other garnishes of your choice.

Serves 8

THE WINE SPECTATOR AWARD

Many of the restaurants included in this cookbook have been recognized by Wine Spectator, the world's most popular wine magazine. It reviews more than 10,000 wines each year and covers travel, fine dining and the lifestyle of wine for novices and connoisseurs alike. Through its Restaurant Awards program, the magazine recognizes restaurants around the world that offer distinguished wine lists.

Awards are given in three tiers. In 2003, more than 3,600 restaurants earned wine list awards. To qualify, wine lists must provide vintages and appellations for all selections. The overall presentation and appearance of the list are also important. Once past these initial requirements, lists are then judged for one of three awards: the Award of Excellence, the Best of Award of Excellence, and the Grand Award.

- **Award of Excellence**—The basic Award of Excellence recognizes restaurants with lists that offer a well-chosen selection of quality producers, along with a thematic match to the menu in both price and style.

- **Best of Award of Excellence**—The second-tier Best of Award of Excellence was created to give special recognition to those restaurants that exceed the requirements of the basic category. These lists must display vintage depth, including vertical offerings of several top wines, as well as excellent breadth from major wine growing regions.

- **Grand Award**—The highest award, the Grand Award, is given to those restaurants that show an uncompromising, passionate devotion to quality. These lists show serious depth of mature vintages, outstanding breadth in their vertical offerings, excellent harmony with the menu, and superior organization and presentation. In 2003, only 89 restaurants held Wine Spectator Grand Awards.

 Award of Excellence    Best of Award of Excellence

 Grand Award

Q Cuisine

2503 Montana Avenue
Billings, MT 59101
406-245-2503
www.qcuisine.com

Reservations recommended
Dinner: Monday – Saturday
4:30 – 10:30 p.m.
Closed on Sundays

Q Cuisine

Michael Schaer, Owner
Suzy Schaer Roberts, General Manager
Daniel Roberts, Executive Chef

Located in downtown Billings on historical Montana Avenue, Q Cuisine is nestled into the first floor of the Carlin Hotel. Built in 1910, the hotel originally catered to first class train passengers arriving at the nearby Billings Depot. The neighborhood and the hotel have been revitalized in recent years. The hotel now offers eight modern and comfortable one-bedroom suites on the third floor, with the second floor leased for office space, and the ground floor housing the Q Cuisine and the Carlin Martini Bar. Guests of the restaurant can enjoy pre- or post-dinner libations in the small intimate Q bar, or in the Carlin Martini Bar.

The award-winning interior design is a stunning mix of historic and contemporary styles. The original 1910 tin ceilings have been given a coat of silver and contrast perfectly with the rich suede panels that cover the walls. Oversized, high back booths in a warm chartreuse line one side of the restaurant and have become as popular as the Bag O' Calamari on the appetizer menu. Along the walls in Q are ten panels of original paintings by Billings' artist, Guy McClelland. The whimsical panels are titled "Deux Couverts, S'il Vous Plait" or "Table for Two, Please", and depict a man enjoying a cocktail, wine and a meal along side his fox terrier dog.

Founded in 2001, Q Cuisine is definitely a family affair. Suzy Schaer serves as the General Manager of the restaurant, which is owned by her father, Michael Schaer. Executive Chef, Daniel Roberts, moved to Billings in 2002, originally working as the pastry chef at Walker's Grill. In February 2003, Roberts was named Executive Chef at Q Cuisine and in April 2005, he married Suzy Schaer. Chef Roberts interest in the culinary arts started at age ten. Raised in New Orleans, the youngest of 12 children, Chef Roberts helped his mother with her Southern Creole-based cooking and assisted his maternal grandmother in running her sweet shop. After attending college at Cal State Long Beach, he traveled and lived abroad for about nine years, tasting the foods of many cultures. His love of cooking led him to enroll in the California School of Culinary Arts, a Cordon Bleu program in Pasadena, graduating in 2001.

You will enjoy Chef Roberts fresh approach to traditional American Bistro cuisine. Along with a wide variety of appetizers and entrees on the menu, you may also have a chance to partake of the Chef's Tasting Menu. It consists of three or four small portion courses determined by the Chef. The tasting menus change daily and take your taste buds through a true dining experience. Along with the sumptuous cuisine, you will be treated to impeccable and professional service throughout your meal.

Spinach Ravioli with Oregon White Truffles

Ingredients

2 pounds spinach, steamed and chopped	Ravioli Dough (recipe follows)
1½ cups ricotta cheese	egg wash
1 tablespoon roasted garlic, crushed	Oregon White Truffle Sauce (recipe
1 egg yolk	follows)
salt and pepper to taste	grated Romano cheese

Preparation

IN A bowl, combine the spinach, ricotta, garlic, and egg yolk. Season the mixture with salt and pepper to taste.

PLACE a pasta square on a lightly floured surface and add 3 tablespoons of the spinach mixture in the center. Brush the pasta with a little egg wash and fold over. Repeat process until you have 12 ravioli. Boil ravioli in salted water for 7 to 8 minutes. Drain ravioli and place in warm bowls. Heat Oregon White Truffle Sauce over high heat until it starts to bubble. Pour the sauce over the ravioli and sprinkle grated Romano cheese over top.

Serves 6 as an entrée or 12 as an appetizer

For the Ravioli Dough

2 cups sifted all purpose flour	¾ cup egg whites
pinch sea salt	1 tablespoon extra virgin olive oil

MIX the flour and salt together. Add all other ingredients and mix until a soft ball is formed. Turn dough out onto a floured surface and kneed for 5 minutes. Cover with plastic and refrigerate for 30 minutes. Roll out squares measuring 5 inches by 5 inches, and ¹⁄₁₆ inch thick.

Yield 12 raviolis

For the Oregon White Truffle Sauce

6 ounces butter	4 ounces heavy cream
1 ounce Oregon white truffles	1 tablespoon white truffle oil

MELT butter over low heat with the truffles. Place in a blender and purée for 1 minute. Add heavy cream and truffle oil. Pulse the mixture a few times. Set aside.

Yield ¾ to 1 cup

Four Peppercorn Encrusted Angus Tenderloin

with Rosemary and Port Demi

Ingredients

2½ pounds Angus tenderloin, cut into 6 to 7-ounce portions
     salt and pepper
     olive oil
¾   cup mixed peppercorns – black, red, green, white
1   pound baby white potatoes, steamed

     butter
1- 2 garlic cloves, sliced thin
1   pound trimmed green asparagus, steamed
     Rosemary and Port Demi Sauce (recipe follows)

Preparation

HEAT grill for 20 minutes on high and heat oven to 400 degrees. Place peppercorns in a spice mill and pulse lightly just to break up peppercorns. Season the tenderloin steaks with a salt and pepper, and then brush with a little olive oil. Firmly press both sides of steaks into the cracked peppercorns. Grill steaks for 3 minutes per side and place in the 400-degree oven for 3 to 5 minutes for medium-rare to medium.

WHILE steaks are on the grill, heat a little butter and the sliced garlic in a saucepan. Add steamed potatoes and cook for 2 minutes or until potatoes are hot. Season with salt and pepper. Add asparagus to pan and set aside, keeping warm.

TO SERVE, place the tenderloin in the center of the plate with the potatoes off center. Put asparagus between the two. Spoon a little of the sauce on top of the tenderloin and around the plate.

Serves 6

For the Rosemary and Port Demi Sauce

3   shallots, sliced
    olive oil
1   cup port wine

1   sprig fresh rosemary
2   ounces cold butter, cubed
    salt and pepper to taste

OVER medium heat, sauté the shallots in a little olive oil. Remove from heat and deglaze the pan with the port wine. Return to heat, bring to a boil and add the sprig of rosemary. Reduce the port by two-thirds. Remove rosemary and swirl in the cubed butter. Season to taste with salt and pepper. Keep warm.

MIXED BERRY PARFAIT

Ingredients

2 cups mixed fresh berries (blueberry, raspberry, blackberry, chopped strawberry)

1 cup Ginger and Anise Simple Syrup (recipe follows)

3 cups low fat yogurt, drained for 1 hour through cheesecloth

2 tablespoons wild flower honey
caramelized almonds, for garnish
fresh mint sprigs, for garnish

Preparation

TOSS fresh berries in the Ginger and Anise Simple Syrup and let sit for at least 1 hour. Drain.

LINE up 8 martini glasses and place 2 tablespoons of the berries in the bottom of each glass. Whisk the honey into the drained yogurt. Pour an even layer of the yogurt mixture over berries – approximately ½ inch thick. Add 3 more tablespoons of berries over the surface to create the next layer. Pour another layer of yogurt on top. Chill before serving. Garnish with the caramelized almonds and fresh mint sprigs.

Serves 8

For the Ginger and Anise Simple Syrup

1 tablespoon fresh ginger, minced
2 whole anise pods

1 cup granulated sugar
1 cup water

BRING the mixture to a boil and turn off heat. Let sit until it cools.

Yield 2 cups

A Rånge Rider of the Yellowstone, posed by William S. Hart and his horse.
By C.C. Cristadoro

The Granary

1500 Poly Dr
Billings, MT 59102
(406) 259-3488

Dining Room:
5:00 p.m. – Close Daily
Bar: 4:00 p.m. – Close Daily

The Granary

Aaron Sparboe,
Jennifer and John Scott, Owners
John Beckner, General Manager
Alan Sparboe, Chef

The Granary has been serving the Billings dining scene for three decades, but a major change occurred in 2004 that has brought this restaurant back to the forefront for those who enjoy fine dining. A major transformation of the building was done, giving the diners a much more intimate experience, and Chef Alan Sparboe has created a menu that features innovative cuisine including many fresh seafood dishes as well as top quality meats. Located across from Rocky Mountain College, the restaurant sits in a lush setting of old trees and lush lawns, with the rimrocks as its backdrop.

Built in 1935, the building was originally used as the milling department for Billings Polytechnic Institute. Students from the Institute, now Rocky Mountain College, earned money producing flour, cereal, and pancake flour. The mill was operated until World War II, at which time it was closed and the building stood idle until 1976, when it was reopened as The Granary Restaurant. The restaurant's main dining room originally featured a lofty ceiling, and an outdoor patio featuring a large old shade tree was added in 1990. The 2004 renovation included lowering the ceiling of the dining room to facilitate a much more intimate setting conducive to quiet conversations. The feeling of an old mill is maintained with the old timber beams throughout the dining room and the lavish use of dark wood in the bar on the main floor. An extensive wine cellar has also been added, which gives diners a wide variety of quality wine from which to choose.

Chef Alan Sparboe completed a two-year course at the New England Culinary Institute. After working at restaurants in Chicago, he returned to Billings where he has worked at the Billings Petroleum Club, Jakes, and the Beanery. As Executive Chef at The Granary, Chef Sparboe has blended some of the favorites of the old restaurant, such as the French Onion Soup and the great steaks, with his love of fresh seafood. His combinations of flavors are exquisite; such as the potato encrusted salmon that sits atop a salad made with fresh fennel, pears, and napa cabbage, and drizzled with anisette beurre blanc. Whatever your tastes, you are likely to find a meal that will please you at The Granary.

BACON WRAPPED SEA SCALLOPS

with Thai Orange Vinaigrette and Citrus Couscous

Ingredients

18 u10 sea scallops, defooted
18 slices honey cured bacon
     Citrus Couscous (recipe follows)

Thai Orange Vinaigrette (recipe
follows)
fresh chives, chopped - for garnish

Preparation

WRAP each scallop with a slice of bacon and skewer on individual metal skewers. In a hot skillet, fry the scallops until the bacon is crisp, about 4-1/2 minutes.

TO SERVE, heat the Citrus Couscous and press into a ring mold. Invert the mold onto a plate. Place the scallops in the center of the ring. Drizzle with the Thai Orange Vinaigrette, and garnish with fresh chives.

Serves 6

For the Citrus Couscous

1   cup chicken stock
½   cup orange juice concentrate

1   teaspoon cilantro, chopped
2   cups couscous

IN A saucepan, heat the stock and orange juice concentrate, and then add the cilantro. Stir in the couscous and cook until tender.

For the Thai Orange Vinaigrette

32   ounces orange juice concentrate
⅛   cup ginger, minced
⅛   cup garlic, minced
½   cup rice wine vinegar

½   tablespoon crushed red chili flakes
2   tablespoons sugar
1   cup olive oil
     salt and pepper to taste

IN A food processor or blender, blend together the orange juice concentrate, ginger, garlic, vinegar, crushed chili flakes, and sugar. Leave the processor on and carefully add the oil to emulsify. Season with salt and pepper. Refrigerate until ready to use.

Yield 3 cups

POTATO WRAPPED SHRIMP
with Saffron Risotto —Strawberry Chipotle Sauce and Mango-Strawberry Salsa

Ingredients

18 *u12 shrimp*
1 *russet potato, peeled and cut into 18 spiral cuts*
oil for deep frying
½ *recipe Saffron Risotto (recipe follows)*

Mango-Strawberry Salso (recipe follows)
Strawberry Chipotle Sauce (recipe follows)
cilantro leaves for garnish

Preparation

WRAP shrimp with a spiral cut of potato to look like mummies. Deep fry until golden brown.

TO SERVE, place a small mound of Saffron Risotto in the center of a pasta bowl. Intertwine 3 shrimp and place on top of risotto. Spoon small amount of Mango-Strawberry Salsa on top, and drizzle Strawberry Chipotle Sauce around edge. Garnish with a cilantro leaf.

For Saffron Risotto

4 *ounces butter*
½ *cup olive oil*
¼ *pound yellow onion, minced*
3 *saffron threads*

4 *pounds Arborio rice*
1 *gallon chicken stock*
1 *cup Parmesan or Asiago cheese, shredded*

HEAT butter and oil in a large heavy-bottomed saucepot. Add onion and saffron threads and sauté until tender, without browning. Add rice and sauté until well coated with butter-onion mixture. Add stock, one ladle at a time, until each ladle is absorbed, stirring constantly.

ADD cheese to finish when ready serve.

Serves 12

For the Strawberry Chipotle Sauce

1 *pint strawberries, less 4 strawberries reserved for salsa recipe*
2 *chipotle peppers*
1 *teaspoon cilantro, chopped*

3 *tablespoons honey*
¼ *cup smoky-flavored barbeque sauce*
1 *tablespoon sugar*
salt and pepper to taste

PLACE all ingredients, except the salt and pepper, into a food processor. Pulse until well incorporated. Adjust seasoning with salt, pepper, and more sugar, if needed. Set aside until ready to serve.

For the Strawberry–Mango Salsa

4 strawberries, diced (reserved from
   strawberry chipotle sauce recipe)
1 mango, diced
½ shallot, diced

1 teaspoon cilantro, chopped
1 tablespoon sugar
2 tablespoons rice wine vinegar
   salt and pepper to taste

PLACE the strawberries, mango, shallot, and cilantro in a bowl and mix with the sugar and vinegar. Adjust the sugar and vinegar to your taste, and season with salt and pepper. Set aside until ready to serve.

Yield 2 cups

CITRUS PINE NUT RISOTTO

This is a great recipe for any leftover risotto that you may have.

Ingredients

3 ounces pre-made risotto
1 tablespoon olive oil
1 tablespoon pine nuts
1 teaspoon citrus zest

½ cup orange juice, reduced to syrup
   consistency
   salt and pepper to taste
1 ounce Parmesan cheese, shredded

Preparation

HEAT a small sauté pan with a tablespoon of olive oil. Add risotto and stir until warmed through. Add pine nuts and zest, stirring to combine. Mix in the orange juice reduction.

FINISH with the Parmesan cheese and serve immediately.

Serves 1

POTATO ENCRUSTED SALMON
with Fennel Pear Salad and Anisette Beurre Blanc

Ingredients

6 8-ounce salmon fillets	salt and pepper to taste
2 russet potatoes, shredded	olive oil
1 egg	Fennel Pear Salad (recipe follows)
½ cup heavy cream	Anisette Beurre Blanc (recipe follows)
2 tablespoons fresh herbs of your choice	fresh herbs or sliced pears for garnish

HEAT the oven to 375 degrees.

IN A mixing bowl, place the shredded potato and mix in the egg, cream, herbs, and salt and pepper to taste. Drain and squeeze out excess liquid. Cover each salmon fillet with a layer of the potato mixture.

IN A hot sauté pan, pour a small amount of olive to coat the bottom. Brown the salmon, potato side down for approximately 4 minutes. Place in 375-degree oven until medium, about 6 minutes.

TO SERVE, place a mound of the Fennel Pear Salad in the center of 6 dinner plates. Top each with a salmon fillet. Drizzle the Anisette Beurre Blanc around the edge. Garnish with chopped fresh herbs or slices of pear arranged in a fan.

For the Fennel Pear Salad

1 fennel bulb, julienned	½ head napa cabbage, cut into ½-inch
2 pears, julienned	shreds
olive oil	salt and pepper to taste

IN A large bowl, mix the fennel, pear, and cabbage. In a large sauté pan, sauté the mixture in a little olive oil until tender. Season the mixture with salt and pepper.

For the Anisette Beurre Blanc

4 star anise	½ pound fennel with fronds, sliced
3 cinnamon sticks	½ cup anisette liquor
4 sprigs fresh thyme	3 tablespoons cream
2 teaspoons black peppercorns	3 pounds butter, cubed and softened
2 garlic cloves	salt and pepper to taste
1 shallot, sliced	

IN A large sauté pan, sauté the star anise, cinnamon sticks, thyme, peppercorns, garlic, shallot, and fennel until the oils release. Deglaze the pan with anisette and simmer until reduced by half. Add the cream and reduce again. Remove from heat and slowly add butter, stirring until totally incorporated. Adjust the seasoning with salt and pepper and strain through a fine strainer. Keep warm until ready to serve.

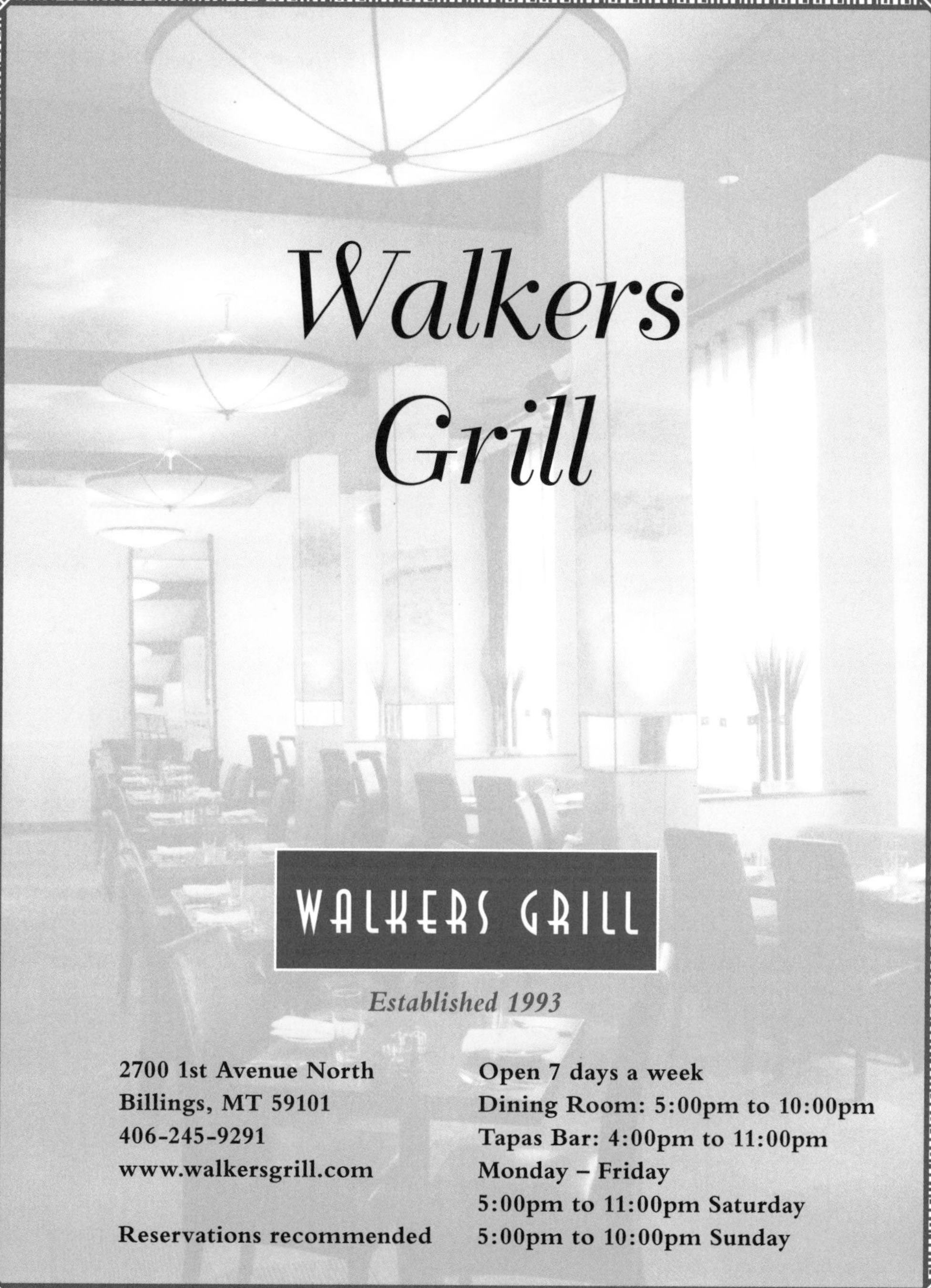

Walkers Grill

WALKERS GRILL

Established 1993

2700 1st Avenue North
Billings, MT 59101
406-245-9291
www.walkersgrill.com

Reservations recommended

Open 7 days a week
Dining Room: 5:00pm to 10:00pm
Tapas Bar: 4:00pm to 11:00pm
Monday – Friday
5:00pm to 11:00pm Saturday
5:00pm to 10:00pm Sunday

Walkers Grill

William Honaker, Owner
Michael Harmon, Chef/Partner

Walkers Grill originally opened in February 1993 in the historic Old Chamber of Commerce building in downtown Billings and could rightly be credited with starting a culinary revolution in this old West frontier town that now boasts several gourmet restaurants. At the start of its second decade, the owners of Walkers Grill purchased the historic five-story Securities Building in the heart of city center, and moved the restaurant into the ground floor of the building.

Located between the Sheraton and Northern hotels, the 145-seat restaurant includes a full bar, and is a well-established local favorite and a destination for travelers, theater-goers, and museum patrons alike. A professional wait staff contributes friendly service in a casual, yet elegant urban setting. The new contemporary Montana feel includes a "grazing bar" or tapas bar, which entails a large selection of hot and cold small plates of sophisticated foods from around the world.

Walkers Grill has been a recipient of the Award of Excellence by Wine Spectator since 1995. It has served such noted guests as Mel Gibson, Lou Gosset, Jr., Jon Voight, Garrison Keillor, Joan Baez, poet Allan Ginsberg, and former President Bill Clinton. The award winning décor of the new Walkers Grill is a unique blend of hip contemporary design and old West everyday furnishings. Photographer Dennis Kern took pictures of the fluffy clouds that float over Montana and had them made into wallpaper for the ceiling, personifying one of the Big Sky Country's most famous symbols. His photos taken between Billings and Red Lodge adorn the light shades. Billings artist, Gordon McConnell, created the romantic black and white murals of cowboys herding horses that decorate the upper walls above the kitchen. The bar continues the western theme with a cattle guard as its base, and light fixtures fashioned out of barbed wire.

All of this splendor does not overpower the exquisite quality of the eclectic cuisine. Walkers Famous Bourbon Street Pasta, topped with Andouille sausage, shrimp, and roasted chicken turns Italian pasta into a masterpiece of Creole cooking. The James Beard Meatloaf has been on the menu almost from the inception of the restaurant and is a favorite of locals. The Slow Pork Osso Bucco is a mouth-watering take on the classic veal dish, and the Peking-Style Duck in its Asian-spiced marinade is another bright star on the menu. The tapas menu is a delightful way to graze through dinner, or you can substitute hot or cold tapas for your soup or salad for a small extra charge. Be sure to save room for one of the sumptuous desserts, or split a Dessert Sampler, which features three of the nightly desserts.

POTATO AND ARTICHOKE GRATIN

Ingredients

    3 eggs
1½ cups heavy cream
       salt and freshly ground pepper to taste
1½ pounds Idaho potatoes, skin on and
       sliced very thin
1½ pounds canned artichokes, drained
       and sliced very thin

1½ cups cheese, grated – a combination
       of your choice
    5 fresh sage leaves, chopped

Preparation

HEAT oven to 350 degrees. In a small bowl, combine eggs and cream; season with salt and pepper. In the bottom of a lightly greased 9" x 12" pan, alternately layer the sliced potatoes and artichokes. Season with salt and pepper and sprinkle with grated cheese and chopped sage every few layers. Continue until pan is full. Pour egg mixture over layered dish and press down to ensure it soaks down to all layers. Cover and bake in a 350-degree oven until tender, about 45 minutes. Serve immediately. You can also place pan in refrigerator to let cool, and then reheat when ready to serve.

Serves 7 to 10

Crusted Venison Loins with Loganberry Sage Sauce

Ingredients

24 ounces venison loin, cut into 4 pieces
salt and pepper to taste
cornmeal grits mixture

olive or other cooking oil
Loganberry Sage Sauce (recipe follows)

Preparation

SEASON the venison loins with salt and pepper. Roll in cornmeal grits mixture to crust. In a sauté pan, sear the loins in a little oil until medium rare. Do not overcook.

TO SERVE, ladle Loganberry Sage Sauce onto plate. Slice each loin into several medallions and arrange over sauce.

For the Loganberry Sage Sauce

1 cup red wine
2 medium shallots, minced
3 cups loganberries
1 cup veal or game stock

1 tablespoon honey
salt and pepper to taste
2 sprigs fresh sage

IN A saucepan, reduce wine and shallot until almost all the liquid is absorbed. Add berries and cook until softened. Add stock, honey, salt and pepper and cook until it coats the back of a spoon. Strain sauce. Add sage and let it infuse sauce for about 15 minutes. Remove sage and keep warm.

Serves 4

Wine suggestion: 1999 Dunham Cellars Cabernet Sauvignon – Walla Walla, WA

Bourbon Street Pasta

Ingredients

1 pound Andouille sausage, cut into half-moons	¼ teaspoon celery salt
olive oil	3 teaspoons gumbo filé
2 red bell peppers, diced large	½ teaspoon cayenne pepper
1 green bell pepper, diced large	⅛ cup Worcestershire sauce
1 yellow onion, chopped	1⅓ cups white wine
1 rib celery, diced fine	10 ounces beef broth
¼ head fresh garlic, minced	10 ounces chicken broth
½–2 Scotch bonnet peppers, minced	salt and pepper to taste
1 cup (plus) tomato stricia* or tomato purée	minced cilantro to taste
½ tablespoon ground cumin	penne or linguini pasta, cooked to taste

Preparation

IN A large stockpot, sauté sausage with a small amount of olive oil. Add bell peppers, onion, celery, and garlic. Add Scotch bonnet peppers to taste; stir to combine. Continue cooking until peppers become slightly tender.

ADD tomato stricia, seasonings, Worcestershire sauce, and white wine, and allow to simmer for about 5 minutes. Add the broths, stirring to combine, and season to taste with salt and pepper. Bring to a boil and then remove from heat. Add minced cilantro to taste after cooling slightly.

TOSS with cooked pasta and serve.

Serves 8

*Tomato stricia is a canned product (available from Sysco) of California ripened tomato strips packed in tomato purée. Can substitue other canned tomato purée.

SEARED DUCK BREASTS
with Duck Sauce Marionberry

Ingredients

    4 duck breasts
    1 tablespoon olive oil
       Duck Sauce Marionberry (recipe follows)

Preparation

IN A sauté pan, add olive oil and bring to high heat. Place duck breasts in sauté pan with fatty side down. Sear breasts, turn and sear other side to medium rare. Let rest for 5 minutes.

TO SERVE, slice and fan duck breasts on plates. Drizzle with Duck Sauce Marionberry

Serves 4

For the Duck Sauce Marionberry

    1 pound marionberries   1 cup sugar
    4 tablespoons fresh ginger, minced 1 can chicken broth
    4 tablespoons shallots, minced   cornstarch, to thicken if desired
    1 cup sherry vinegar

COMBINE the marionberries, ginger, shallots, vinegar, and sugar in a saucepan, and bring to a boil. Reduce until very syrupy. Add broth and bring back to a boil. Sprinkle in cornstarch to thicken, if desired. Adjust seasonings, and run through finest blade on a food mill. Set aside and keep warm.

WALKERS APPLE CRISP

Ingredients

4-6 Granny Smith apples, peeled and
    sliced
¼ cup lemon juice
¾ cup granulated sugar
½ cup brown sugar

1 cup flour
½ teaspoon cinnamon
½ teaspoon salt
¼ cup butter, cut into small squares and
    softened

Preparation

HEAT oven to 350 degrees. Combine apples, lemon juice and granulated sugar and press mixture evenly into a 9 x 12 (4-inch deep) baking dish.

COMBINE the rest of the ingredients in a mixer with a paddle at medium speed. Mix until topping breaks into small crumbles. Add topping to apple mixture, packing loosely. Bake at 350 degrees for 45 minutes to 1 hour.

Walkers Grill, Billings

VENISON LOVERS!

Research shows that humans have been eating venison for 50,000 years. At an early point in time, man was even culling excess young male ungulates so the breeding herd would continue to flourish. (Diggers have found a preponderance of young male deer bones in caves). Westerners changed their diet beginning around 1600 when cattle, sheep, hogs, and goats became the domestic meat resource of choice because they had all that marvelous fat for keeping us warm and burning the midnight oil.

When you think of "venison," the deer species comes to mind, but did you know that venison can refer to the flesh of any big game animal used as food?

Today, many cooks are afraid to prepare venison because they have heard about its alleged dryness, toughness, and unpleasant flavor. Cooking your venison is very easy, once a few basic harvesting and cooking procedures have been learned. It contains only 3 to 5 percent fat (compared to beef at 20 percent fat) and almost no cholesterol.

Venison is a fine, delicately textured meat. Many cuts are very similar to veal. Other cuts, such as chops, look like pork. Round steaks, although smaller, have the appearance of beef. Stew meat and ground venison also resemble beef. Even though many cuts of venison look like other meats, venison has one characteristic that makes it unique. Since venison is a low or no fat-meat, during cooking it needs additional moisture.

If you purchase non-native species of venison (like axis, fallow, or red deer) or commercial elk that have been harvested and processed under state or USDA Inspections, you have no concerns about the quality of your meat. Commercial animals are thoroughly inspected for health at the time of harvest.

If you do not hunt or do not have a ready access to domestic venison, you may find farms in your area in the Yellow Pages that raise and ship venison; or go to culinary sources in the back of this book to find mail-order sources. Since it is illegal to buy, sell, or trade in deer species that are native to the United States, these ranchers have imported European, Australian, or Asian deer and bred them specifically for this market. These suppliers are USDA inspected and they will be able to provide you with the exact cuts of venison that you require. Some of these firms also market prepared venison products. Other firms have fresh venison air-shipped daily from New Zealand and Europe.

Whether we want to eat healthy chemical-free meat or we need to cut back our caloric intake, we're coming back to natural, fat-free, venison. Some say it is the meat of the 21st Century.

Chico Hot Springs

Established 1900

#1 Chico Road
Pray, MT 59065
1-800-HOT-WADA or 406-333-4933
www.chicohotsprings.com
chico@chicohotsprings.com

Open year-round
Nightly, 5:30 to 9:00 pm – fall and winter
5:30 to 10:00 p.m. – spring and summer
Sunday brunch, served from
8:30 am to 11:30 am
Reservations recommended

Chico Hot Springs

Eve & Mike Art, Owners
Colin Davis, General Manager
Chris Clark, Chef

The area that is known today as Chico Hot Springs got its commercial start during the territorial period when miners stopped by to bathe and "wash their duds". Prior to that, native peoples had long appreciated its soothing waters. In 1876, an inventive settler tapped into the 112-degree water, piping it under his greenhouse to grow vegetables for local residents. In 1894, Percie and Bill Knowles inherited the property and ran a boarding house for miners. They built a hot springs hotel in 1900, but when Bill Knowles died in 1910, Percie and her son, Radbourne, turned the luxurious hotel into a respected medical facility, gaining renown throughout the Northwest. After Radbourne's death in 1943, Chico Hot Springs went through a series of owners until Mike and Eve Art purchased the property in 1973 and, through the years, have restored the resort to its former glory. Today, the property consists of three lodges, a saloon (live bands every Friday and Saturday night), a day spa, a gift shop, an activity center, a full convention facility, and a horse barn.

With its Georgian-inspired architecture and warm Craftsman-style interiors, Chico is one of Montana's best-preserved examples of an early 20th century hot springs hotel and health resort. In June 1999, Chico was listed on the National Register of Historic Places.

The dining room specializes in fresh, exceptional cuisine, with most of the produce coming from Chico's own garden. The steaks are generous, the seafood in flown in fresh, and all of the baking is done on the premises. Chico boasts one of the region's finest wine cellars, with the wine list receiving the Wine Spectator Award of Excellence six times.

As well as being a favorite of the locals, Chico is also a choice of many of Montana's Hollywood contingent, including Peter Fonda, Jeff Bridges, and Dennis Quaid. In the old days, Chico even hosted famed cowboy artist Charlie Russell, who traded drawings on the back of stationary for drinks. President Theodore Roosevelt also stayed at the resort the night before he visited Yellowstone National Park.

Award of Excellence

CHICO HOT SPRINGS

ROASTED RED PEPPER SOUP

The earthy flavors of roasted red peppers bring out the savory freshness of this soup. The color is a vibrant red that makes any table stunning. This soup is versatile enough to be paired with a variety of other ingredients. Try steamed mussels, clams, or other shellfish as a last-minute topping. Prepare the chicken stock a day in advance.

Ingredients

6 - 8 large red bell peppers
2 quarts (64 ounces) Chicken Stock (recipe follows)
canola oil to coat pan
2 large yellow onions, sliced for sautéing
1 large carrot, rough diced
4 large shallots, rough diced
4 cups canned tomatoes with juice, or 6 large tomatoes, peeled and seeded
4 stalks celery, rough diced

2 cloves garlic, rough diced
1 cup sherry, divided
1 cup heavy whipping cream
¼ teaspoon saffron
juice of 1 lemon
½ teaspoon of your favorite hot sauce (optional)
salt and pepper to taste
½ cup freshly grated Parmesan cheese

Preparation

ROAST whole red bell peppers over an open flame on a gas burning stovetop or grill. Remove from flame when skin is mostly blackened and immerse in an ice bath to remove skin easily. Seed and dice. Peppers can also be roasted in a 400-degree oven for 10 to 20 minutes. Set aside.

IN A large soup pot, warm the chicken stock on medium-high heat until boiling. Add roasted red peppers; let simmer.

HEAT a saucepan with canola oil and sauté onions, carrot, shallots, tomatoes, celery, and garlic until browned. Add ½ cup of the sherry to vegetables, deglazing the pan. Stir and combine with hot chicken stock. On medium-high heat allow mixture to reduce to half, about 1-½ hours, stirring occasionally.

PUREE mixture in a blender or food processor until smooth. Return to soup pot on low heat. Whisk in heavy whipping cream, saffron, lemon juice, remaining ½ cup sherry, and the optional hot sauce. Add salt and pepper to taste, simmer for 10 minutes, and serve with freshly grated Parmesan cheese sprinkled over top.

Serves 4

ROASTED RED PEPPER SOUP, CONTINUED

For the Chicken Stock

1 small whole chicken (about 3 pounds)	1 bunch parsley or stems, rough chopped
1 whole duck (4 to 5 pounds)	3 bay leaves
3 large carrots, rough chopped	1 tablespoon black peppercorns
6 stalks celery, rough chopped	2 tablespoons kosher salt
2 large white onions, rough chopped	
4 cloves garlic, rough chopped	

PLACE chicken and duck with organs and necks in a large (3-gallon) stockpot; add other ingredients. Fill with cold water just to cover the ingredients. Simmer over medium heat for 6 to 12 hours. Skim fat off top and strain. Stock keeps up to 3 days in refrigerator. If not used by then, it should be frozen or discarded.

Yields 6 quarts

Tomato-Basil Bruschetta

Using fresh basil and tomatoes from the Chico garden or greenhouse, this appetizer is a favorite throughout the year. The three different sauces used in the recipe add layers of fresh flavor, putting a new spin on this classic Italian dish.

Ingredients

2 loaves French bread
  Goat Cheese Spread (recipe follows)
½ cup freshly grated Parmesan cheese
  Tomato and Basil Salsa (recipe follows)

½ cup Balsamic Vinegar Reduction Sauce (recipe follows)
½ cup Basil Oil (recipe follows)

Preparation

HEAT oven to 450 degrees. Cut bread at an angle into 1-inch thick slices. Generously spread Goat Cheese Spread on each slice and place on a baking sheet. Sprinkle half of the Parmesan cheese on the slices and bake until golden brown, about 5 minutes.

WHILE bread is still hot, top with Tomato-Basil Salsa and sprinkle with remaining Parmesan cheese. Drizzle Balsamic Vinegar Reduction Sauce and Basil Oil alternately over Bruschetta and serve.

Serves 4 to 6

For the Goat Cheese Spread

2 ounces goat cheese
4 tablespoons (½ stick) unsalted butter
½ teaspoon powdered mustard

1 teaspoon Worcestershire sauce
¼ teaspoon granulated onion
1 teaspoon fresh chives, chopped

IN A small bowl, mix all ingredients together until thoroughly combined and smooth.

For Tomato-Basil Salsa

15 Roma tomatoes, seeds removed, and diced
3 tablespoons extra virgin olive oil
3 tablespoons balsamic vinegar

2 tablespoons minced garlic
½ tablespoon salt
4 tablespoons fresh basil, julienned

HEAT oven to 400 degrees. Mix tomatoes, olive oil, vinegar, garlic, and salt together. Spread mixture evenly on a baking sheet and roast in the oven for 8 to 10 minutes. Remove from oven and let cool. When cool, add basil and toss.

For the Balsamic Vinegar Reduction Sauce

>   2 cups balsamic vinegar

IN A saucepan, reduce vinegar over medium heat until it forms a syrup, about 20 minutes. If it coats a spoon, the sauce is done.

Yields ½ cup

For the Basil Oil

>   1 cup fresh basil, packed without stems
>   ½ cup grape seed oil (canola oil can be substituted)
>   12-inch piece of cheesecloth

BLANCH basil in boiling water for 10 seconds. Remove and shock in ice water. Pat basil dry with paper towels. It is important to dry the leaves thoroughly; water will make the oil separate. Combine basil and oil in a blender and blend for 30 seconds. Strain the mixture through cheesecloth; do not squeeze.

Yields ¼ to ½ cup

Raspberry Chocolate Decadence Truffle Torte

In the restaurant we use garden-picked raspberries to temper the absolute richness of this flourless torte. Serve with semisweet chocolate shavings, Crème Anglaise, and 3 fresh whole raspberries for garnish. For a simpler accent, serve with fresh whipped cream.

Ingredients

1 cup fresh raspberries small amount of melted butter	¼ teaspoon raspberry oil (optional) 6 eggs
1 pound bittersweet chocolate, chopped into small pieces	Crème Anglais (recipe follows)
½ pound (2 sticks) unsalted butter, cubed	30 fresh raspberries, for garnish semisweet chocolate shavings, for garnish

Preparation

PUREE the cup of raspberries using a blender or food processor on high speed. When finished, you should have about ¾ cup of a thick, smooth liquid.

PREHEAT over to 450 degrees. Prepare a 9-inch springform pan by brushing with melted butter. Line bottom of pan with a parchment circle and brush with melted butter. Wrap foil around outside bottom and sides of the pan. Place in a large pan filled with 1 inch of water. The foil will prevent any water seepage into the springform pan.

MELT the chocolate and unsalted butter over a double boiler until smooth. Add raspberry oil if you are using it and stir thoroughly. Remove from heat. Place eggs in a separate bowl and place over the same simmering water used for the chocolate; whisk eggs until they are warm to the touch. Pour eggs into mixer and whip until tripled in volume. With a rubber spatula, fold whipped eggs into the chocolate mixture in thirds until incorporated and smooth.

POUR chocolate mixture into prepared springform pan and spoon the raspberry puree into the mixture in a circle pattern; swirl with a sharp knife. Bake for 5 minutes at 450 degrees. Reduce oven temperature to 375 degrees and cover pan with foil. Bake 10 more minutes. Cake will look very soft. Remove from oven and take springform pan out of water. Remove foil, and let cool for 30 minutes. Refrigerate overnight.

TO REMOVE cake from pan, place entire pan over a burner with a very low flame. Rotate pan over flame for 15 seconds. Remove cake from springform and invert onto a plate. Remove parchment and invert onto another plate.

PLACE torte slices on individual dessert plates and serve with Crème Anglais, a few chocolate shavings and 3 fresh raspberries on top.

Serves 10

For the Crème Anglaise

3 egg yolks
⅓ cup sugar, plus 2 tablespoons

1 cup half-and-half
1 teaspoon pure vanilla extract

COMBINE egg yolks and sugar; whip until light and fluffy. In a saucepan, bring half-and-half to a slight boil; gently fold in yolk mixture. Place on a double boiler over simmering water until the mixture reaches between 180 to 190 degrees, not above. Sauce is done when it coats the back of a spoon.

STIR IN vanilla extract, transfer to a bowl or small pitcher. Let cool to room temperature and refrigerate until ready to serve.

Yields 1 cup

HERB CRUSTED FILET MIGNON WITH PORT WINE SAUCE

Ingredients

¼ cup fennel seeds
¼ cup whole coriander seeds
1 teaspoon salt

1 teaspoon black pepper
4 beef tenderloin steaks, 8 ounces each
 Port Wine Sauce (recipe follows)

Preparation

IN A spice grinder or blender, pulse fennel seeds, coriander seeds, salt, and pepper until coarsely ground. Roll outer edge of each steak in herbs to form a crust; do not encrust cut ends. Grill each steak to desired temperature: 6 to 8 minutes per side for Medium Rare and 14 to 18 minutes on each side for Medium Well.

LADLE warm Port Wine Sauce unto individual serving plates, making a small pool slightly larger than the steaks. Set steaks on top of the sauce.

For Port Wine Sauce

1½ cups port wine
1 cup sweet vermouth
¼ cup sugar

COMBINE ingredients in a small saucepan. Reduce over medium heat until the mixture forms a syrup, about 30 minutes. If it coats a spoon, the sauce is done. Keep warm until ready to serve.

Serves 4

Adagio Trattoria

101 N. Main Street
Livingston, MT 59047
406-222-7400

Open Monday through Saturday
from 11:00 am until 9:00 pm.
www.livingstonpizza.com

ADAGIO Trattoria

Jim Liska, Owner/Chef

During the day, ADAGIO is a busy lunch spot, offering a wide variety of hot and cold sandwiches, salads and pizzas. In the evening, the intimate 26-seat restaurant serves pasta, salads, pizza, and delicious Italian entrees. Each of the soups at ADAGIO is housemade every morning, as are all of the breads and pizza crusts.

Jim Liska and his wife, Geri Lester, bought the corner pizza parlor in the heart of downtown Livingston in 2004 and slowly began turning it into a full-blown Italian restaurant. Though Jim has no formal training as a cook, except for a weekend course he took in Los Angeles to learn to make sushi, he had been constantly urged by his dinner guests to open his own restaurant. His culinary training came from learning how to prepare Italian cuisine from his Sicilian "Uncle" Joe and "Grandma" Interlandi when he was growing up in Chicago.

A career journalist and jazz critic for the Los Angeles Times, Jim has been the editor of the Playboy Jazz Festival magazine since 1980. His passion for cooking is matched only by his passion for music and literature. The very name for the restaurant reflects his musical background. Adagio describes a tempo that is graceful and easy, qualities Jim and Geri like to impart to their guests at the restaurant.

ADAGIO is located in a building that was first a mercantile at the turn of the last century, and then the City Drug Pharmacy from the late 1920s. During prohibition, a speakeasy was operated from the building's basement. The building became Stefano's Pizza around 1990, and in the mid-90s it was known as the Pizza Garden.

The wine list features Italian wines at very reasonable prices, selling them at retail for consumption at the restaurant and also to take out. Food can also be ordered for takeout, but you will experience the full joy of your special meal by sitting in an intimate corner of the restaurant surrounded by the ambiance of a Tuscan bistro.

SALAD ADAGIO

People looking for low-carb food selections don't usually wander into Italian restaurants, where pastas and bread tend to dominate the menu. We met the challenge with this salad, which quickly became one of our top sellers. Even people not watching their waistlines really enjoy this.

Ingredients

- 1 healthy portion of green leaf lettuce
- 3 tablespoons Adagio vinegar mix (equal parts balsamic, red wine vinegar, Chianti)
- 3 ounces pancetta, diced
- 1 tablespoon extra-virgin olive oil
- 1 pinch oregano
- 1 pinch rosemary
- 1 pinch thyme
- 2 eggs, beaten
- 3 tablespoons extra-virgin olive oil, for mixing with greens
- 1 tablespoon diced tomato, as garnish freshly ground pepper

Preparation

PLACE torn lettuce in a bowl and toss with vinegar mix.

In a six-inch skillet, sauté pancetta for 2-3 minutes over high heat. Add 1 tablespoon olive oil and the herbs. After a minute or so, add the eggs and cook until thoroughly cooked.

ADD 3 tablespoons extra-virgin olive oil to the greens and mix. Place in a shallow serving bowl. Divide the egg and pancetta mixture into 3 or 4 pieces and pile on top of the lettuce. Garnish with tomato and freshly ground pepper.

Serves 1

Wine suggestion: Santa Margherita Pinot Grigio

BRACIOLE

My father's best friend, Joe Interlandi, was a physician whose parents were from Sicily. "Uncle" Joe and his mother often cooked side-by-side at big family gatherings. The kitchen was where the action was and it was there I got my first lessons in Italian cooking.

Grandma taught me how to make braciole, putting a stop to incessant questions by reminding me that the only ingredient that mattered was love.

I got to prepare this dish at my home in Los Angeles for Uncle Joe many years later, about a year before he died. He liked it.

Ingredients

1½ pound slice of round steak, ½" inch
   thick
¾ pound ground pork
¼ cup freshly grated Reggiano-
   Parmigiana
1 egg, lightly beaten
2 teaspoons fennel seed
2 cloves garlic, minced
¼ cup chopped Italian parsley
   salt and pepper, to taste

1 tablespoon extra-virgin olive oil
1 tablespoon butter
¾ cup onion, diced
¼ cup celery, diced
¼ cup carrot, diced
1 clove garlic, minced
½ cup red wine
2 tablespoons tomato paste
1 teaspoon oregano
1-2 cups beef stock

Preparation

POUND the steak with a mallet until it is ¼-inch thick. Cut into four equal pieces.

IN A bowl, combine the pork with the cheese, egg, fennel, garlic, parsley and salt and pepper to taste. Divide the mixture into four equal parts and spread over the steak slices. Roll up slices tightly and secure with kitchen twine.

IN A skillet over medium heat, heat the oil and butter and brown the beef rolls. Add onion and cook for 5-6 minutes; add the celery and carrot and cook 2-3 minutes; add garlic and cook for 1 minute; add red wine and cook until it is nearly evaporated. Stir in the tomato paste, oregano and stock and slowly simmer for 45-60 minutes, turning the beef rolls from time to time.

TO SERVE, slice into 1-inch pieces and place over polenta.

Serves 4

Wine suggestions: Allegrini Pallazzo del Torre 2000, Veneto; Boroli Barbera d'Alba 2001, Piemonte

SKILLET ADAGIO

We offer this dish as an occasional lunch special, or if any of our good customers request it. The skillet is a favorite of our friend Margot Kidder. What makes it so tasty is the quality of our sausage: custom-made for us from our own recipe. It is slightly spicy, with plenty of fennel. We also use whatever fresh greens are available on any given day.

Ingredients

extra-virgin olive oil
½ medium onion, diced
1 stalk celery, sliced
4 ounces pre-cooked, crumbled Italian sausage

½ cup diced tomatoes, in their juices
1 cup greens (spinach, escarole, endive, kale)
⅓ cup cannellini beans

Preparation

IN A 12" skillet, over medium-high heat, sauté onion in the oil for 3-4 minutes. Add celery and cook for another minute or two. Add sausage and cook another 2-3 minutes. Add tomatoes and greens, and cook until the greens are somewhat wilted. Add beans and continue to cook until the beans are thoroughly warmed.

PLATE in a shallow bowl and top with fresh-ground pepper. Serve with crusty, hot bread.

Serves 1

Beer suggestion: Peroni Lager or Moretti La Rossa

BRAISED LAMB

Geri grew up on a farm in Galway, Ireland, where "bum" lambs were nurtured back to health next to the warmth of the farmhouse fireplace. As a little girl, she named each of those lambs and, of course, won't eat any of their distant cousins.

I love lamb and was eager to feature a dish that would provide a bowl of hearty comfort in our cold winters.

We feature locally grown, natural lamb from Sterling Lambs, right here in Livingston.

Ingredients

10 anchovy fillets, drained and rinsed	⅓ cup red wine vinegar
1 teaspoon red pepper flakes	1 red bell pepper, cut into 2-inch pieces
extra-virgin olive oil	1 Hungarian wax pepper, cut into 2-inch pieces
3 pounds lamb, cut into 2-inch cubes	
salt & pepper, to taste	4 large garlic cloves, minced
1½ cups dry white wine	1 teaspoon oregano

Preparation

IN A large skillet, combine a small amount of olive oil, the anchovies and red pepper flakes and cook over medium heat for 2-3 minutes.

SEASON the lamb with salt and pepper. Add to the pan and brown, being careful not to crowd the meat in the pan. If necessary, brown the lamb in batches. Season again to taste and add remaining ingredients. Cover and simmer until meat is fork tender, about one hour.

SERVE the lamb and peppers ladled over broken, cooked lasagne noodles or polenta.

Serves 4 to 6

Wine suggestion: Selvapiano Chianti Rufina 2000, Toscana

PEACHES WITH BASIL

We love peaches and nectarines in almost any guise—pies, cobblers, preserves—but when our adventure-writer friend Tim Cahill and his wife, Linnea, invited us to dinner one summer evening, we enjoyed them anew; grilled over hot coals and spooned over ice cream.

At the restaurant the next morning, a batch of peaches, skinned and roughly chopped, ended up in a sauté pan with brown sugar and plenty of butter. We always have plenty of fresh basil and I threw a handful of torn leaves into the pan. The result was fabulous. Spooned over a quality vanilla ice cream, it quickly became our most popular summer desserts.

Ingredients

4 peaches or nectarines
    brown sugar, to taste
6-8 tablespoons butter

5-6 fresh basil leaves
    vanilla ice cream

Preparation

PEEL the fruit and discard the stone. Chop into spoon-size pieces and taste for sweetness, adding brown sugar until desired taste is achieved. Over low heat, sauté the fruit gently in sugar and butter for 6-8 minutes. Add the torn basil leaves and continue cooking until leaves wilt.

SERVE warm over vanilla ice cream.

Serves 4

Wine suggestion: Zardetto Proseco Brut

Covered wagon train, Jerkline 12 on old freight road. (1883)

Second Street Bistro

123 North Second Street
Livingston, MT 59047
(406) 222-WINE (9463)
www.secondstreetbistro.com

Tuesday through Friday: 11:00am until late
Saturday: 5:00pm until late
Sunday Brunch: 10:00am – 2:00pm
Sunday Pizza Night: 5:00pm until late
Closing hours vary with season & day of the week

2nd Street Bistro

John McNaughton & Brian Menges, Owners
Reynolds Lassiter, Chef

Over 100 years old, the Murray Hotel has been a flagship of Livingston, hosting presidents, movie stars and royalty during its long history. Buffalo Bill and Calamity Jane have enjoyed spending time at the Murray. Located across the street from the old Railroad Depot, the elegant old hotel served as the home to Walter Hill, son of the railroad baron, James J. Hill. He and his buddy, Will Rogers, have a history of creating pranks at the hotel. In more recent years, Hollywood director Sam Peckinpah also called the hotel one of his homes.

Located on the ground floor of the hotel, 2nd Street Bistro has become a favorite of locals and visitors since its inception in May 2004 by two partners, John McNaughton and Brian Menges. The partners met each other while running a restaurant in Jackson Hole, Wyoming. It was there that they collaborated on the idea to open a quality-oriented restaurant that embraced the concept and cuisine of a traditional bistro, but with a Montana feel. Their philosophy of bistro cuisine does not rely on specialized ingredients, but rather on specialized technique.

The partners have Chef Reynolds Lassiter on board to execute this philosophy. Chef Lassiter was born and raised in North Carolina. He was trained at the Western Culinary Institute in Portland, Oregon, and has worked at restaurants in New Orleans and Missoula before joining the 2nd Street Bistro.

The delightful lunch and dinner menus will start your taste buds singing as you try to choose between appetizers such as Frog Legs Provencal, Moroccan Lamb Cigarettes, and Trinity Crab Cake. Lunches center on luscious gourmet burgers, as well as soups and salads. Dinners provide you with choices such as the ever popular Homemade Meatloaf, Herb Roasted Chicken, and Coriander Crusted Salmon, and the Sunday brunches offer a wide variety of egg dishes, as well as most of the lunch and dinner appetizers. Available at all times are their bistro pizzas, presenting a gourmet selection along with a pie of the day. The comprehensive wine list offers an array, including some little known wines.

Sunday evenings, the restaurant has a unique concept: Pizza Night. This is a fun time for adventurous pizza lovers, featuring all you can eat pizza and salad, along with wine specials. The kitchen makes enough of one kind of pizza to feed everyone in the dining room. Then it is passed around one slice at a time while another variety of pizza is made.

Second Street Bistro's Seasoned Salt

Seasoned Salt is one of our greatest tricks of the trade. Sometimes the difference between good and great is salt and pepper, and sometimes the difference between great and awesome is seasoned salt and pepper. Use it as a wet rub on red meats, chicken and game. Be careful using it on fish, especially delicate white fish, as it can become overpowering.

Ingredients

1 tablespoon fresh peeled garlic cloves	1 tablespoon fresh thyme
2 tablespoons Italian parsley, chopped	1 tablespoon fresh sage
1 tablespoon fresh rosemary	3 cups kosher salt

Preparation

PROCESS the garlic and herbs in a food processor. Then add the kosher salt, and process until smooth. It should feel like wet beach sand. Store in a glass jar with a tight-fitting lid.

Yield 3⅓ cups

Dining in the cellar at Second Street Bistro.

MEDITERRANEAN FISH STEW

The flavors of the Mediterranean can be found everywhere at the Second Street Bistro: tomatoes, olives, garlic, fine herbs, olive oil. This dish has always been one of my favorites. It is very close to a bouillabaisse, but it is said you can't really make a bouillabaisse outside of Marseilles (even though the best one I've had was in Bandol), so we just call ours Mediterranean Fish Stew. The most important part of this dish is the broth (which is vegetarian) and it is always better if it is made ahead of time and allowed to rest so the flavors can mingle. The choice of fish is wide open, just avoid really oily fish, but most of the fish sold in the United States will work just fine.

Ingredients

3 2-inch by 1-inch pieces of fish of your choice (snapper, salmon, tuna)
4 mussels
2 shrimp
¼ cup raw calamari
1 tablespoon clarified butter

1 teaspoon garlic, chopped
   red chili flakes to taste
⅛ cup Pernod (a French anise-based liquor)
1 cup Vegetarian Broth (recipe follows)

Preparation

HEAT a sauté pan until it is hot and add the butter. Add the fish, mussels, and shrimp and give them a hard sear. When you turn the fish over, add the calamari, garlic and some red chili flakes. Then add the Pernod to deglaze the pan. If you are working over a gas stove, be careful as the liquor may ignite.

POUR the Vegetarian Broth over the seafood, cover and let it simmer until the mussels open and the fish is cooked. Do not overcook.

SERVE in a great big bowl with some grilled bread rubbed with fresh garlic.

Serves 1

For the Vegetarian Broth

1 Spanish onion, cut in chunks	10 roma tomatoes, cut in half
1 fennel bulb, cut in chunks	1 bay leaf
2 garlic cloves	½ teaspoon fresh thyme
olive oil	4 cups water
pinch red chili flakes	4 leaves fresh basil
⅛ teaspoon saffron	

IN A large saucepan, sauté onion, fennel and garlic in olive oil until aromatic. Add chili flakes, saffron, roma tomatoes, bay leaf, and thyme, stirring to combine. Then add about 4 cups of water and let it simmer for half an hour. Remove the bay leaf, add the fresh basil leaves, and give the mixture a rough puree.

Yield about 4 cups

ENDIVE SALAD

This salad is a joy to eat and wonderful to look at. The main thing to keep in mind is that there must be consistency in the thickness of ingredients (especially the apples blending in with the endive). The main concept behind this salad is the bitterness of the endive, playing off of the sweetness of the apples and the spunk of the cheese and nuts. The dressing is very simple, just champagne vinegar and walnut oil.

Ingredients

4 good-sized endives (if they are small use more)	⅛ cup of high quality blue cheese (Maytag, gorgonzola or the like)
1 granny smith apple (de-cored and sliced very thinly to match the endive)	2 tablespoons chopped parsley vinaigrette – a combination of ⅓ champagne vinegar and ⅔ high quality walnut oil
⅛ cup of toasted walnuts (crush them slightly in your hand before adding)	

Preparation

AS WITH all salads, this should be treated with respect. Use a bowl to mix your ingredients. Once all ingredients are together, add the vinaigrette on the side of the bowl (don't just dump it on top of the salad) and gently toss the mixture with your hand. Serve on chilled plates.

Serves 4

THE SECOND STREET BISTRO POLENTA

Ingredients

6 strips apple wood smoked bacon
1 medium onion, diced fine
7 cups chicken stock or broth
7 cups whole milk
4 cups (approximately) stone ground
   white or yellow polenta

1 teaspoon 2nd Street Bistro Seasoned
   Salt (see recipe in this section)
   freshly ground black pepper to taste
1 cup shredded Parmesan Reggiano
1 cup shredded Gruyere

Preparation

START by dicing the bacon finely (using frozen, or very cold bacon makes this easy). Heat a medium sized, heavy-bottomed pot over medium-high heat. When pot is hot, add diced bacon and stir frequently with a wooden spoon.

DO NOT let the bacon become crispy.

WHEN the bacon begins to brown, add the onion and sauté for a couple of minutes until translucent. Add chicken stock and milk. Bring to a boil. Season with salt and pepper.

WHILE stirring constantly with a whisk, add ¾ of the polenta in a steady stream. Lower heat to low and allow mixture to thicken. Let bubble for 2 minutes, being careful not to let it splash on you. Mixture should be thick (the consistency of hot oatmeal). If needed, slowly stir in more polenta until this consistency is achieved. Taste and correct seasoning by adding more seasoned salt and pepper if desired.

REMOVE pot from heat and stir in both cheeses.

POLENTA can be served now as soft polenta, or spread in jellyroll pan and allowed to cool. Spray the pan and use parchment paper (it will help in removing the polenta). In the restaurant, we often cut the cooled polenta into desired shapes, which can be grilled or sautéed for different presentations.

BACON WRAPPED HERBED MEATLOAF

Since the first day that we opened, this has been our top selling dinner entrée. It really embodies the whole concept of the bistro: simple everyday products brought up to a higher level with solid technique. We incorporate a wild mushroom puree, which makes the meatloaf very moist. Meatloaf is something that is made by feel, which makes a definite recipe hard to create.

Ingredients

1 cup wild mushrooms
olive oil
½ cup whole cream
1 pound ground beef
1 pound ground veal
1 pound ground pork
6 eggs
1 small Spanish onion, very finely diced
1 tablespoon fresh thyme, chopped
1 tablespoon parsley, chopped

1 tablespoon garlic, chopped
3 ounces ketchup
2 or 3 dashes Worcestershire sauce
½ cup breadcrumbs
Second Street Bistro Seasoned Salt to taste (see recipe this section)
pepper to taste
raw bacon, enough to cover top and bottom of meatloaf
2 bay leaves

Preparation

SAUTÉ wild mushrooms with a little olive oil, and then add the whole cream and reduce. Cool, and puree the mixture. Set aside.

HEAT oven to 350 degrees. In a large bowl, gently mix together the 3 pounds of ground meat. In another bowl, lightly beat the 6 eggs. Add the onion, thyme, parsley, garlic, ketchup, Worcestershire sauce and combine. Add this mixture to the ground meat, along with the mushroom mixture. Gently combine. Add enough of the breadcrumbs to firm up the mixture.

LINE a meatloaf pan with raw bacon and then fill with the mixture, making sure there are no air pockets. Top the meatloaf with a few more slices of raw bacon and the two bay leaves. Bake in a 350-degree oven until the internal temperature is 140 degrees. When it comes out of the oven let it cool for a bit, then drain off the excess fat. Serve slices of the meatloaf over mashed potatoes.

Serves 6 to 8

Mex John making pies.

Boodles Restaurant

215 East Main
Bozeman, MT 59715
Historic downtown Bozeman
406-587-2901

Reservations recommended
Dinner nightly at 5:30 pm
Nonsmoking

Intimate dining is available in Boodles wine cellar.

Boodles Restaurant

W. Jackson Kent, Owner
Erik J. Nelson, Chef

Boodles is located in the heart of historic Bozeman. When you enter Boodles you are greeted by a warm, comfortable atmosphere, hardwoods, rich fabrics, period art, and a unique 1860s mahogany bar originally crafted in Philadelphia.

Boodles has received the Wine Spectator Award of Excellence for the past four years. They have designed a menu with culinary flair to complement natural flavors and textures. In addition to the creative preparation of the menu they are proud to offer certified handcut Angus beef, seafood, organically grown vegetables, homemade breads and pastries, and other specialties to enhance your dining experience. Whether you are looking for a snack or special dessert after a concert, handcrafted cocktails at Boodles bar, an intimate dining experience, or a private function in their wine cellar, Boodles should be on your list of destinations. As one diner who had moved to Montana from New York recently remarked, "The atmosphere, menu, wine list, and service reminds me of dining in one of New York's finest."

 Award of Excellence

The painting in the main dining area was completed in the 1800's and brought over from Sussex, England.

ROASTED TURKEY SALAD
with Molasses Vinaigrette and Grilled Apples, Currants, and Bacon

Ingredients

2 heads butter lettuce
2 cups arugula
1 cup currants
8 slices bacon, cooked and chopped

4 apples, sliced
Roasted Turkey (recipe follows)
Molasses Vinaigrette (recipe follows)

Preparation

BREAK up lettuce and arugula and place in large bowl. Add currants and bacon, tossing to combine. Add vinaigrette and roasted turkey and toss again.

TO SERVE, arrange apple slices around rim of bowl or plate, placing tossed salad in center.

Serves 4

For the Roasted Turkey

1 4-pound boneless turkey breast
2 tablespoons oil
1 tablespoon salt

1 tablespoon freshly ground pepper
2 teaspoons parsley flakes
2 teaspoons dried oregano

HEAT oven to 400 degrees. Rinse turkey and pat dry. Combine oil and spices and rub turkey with mixture. Place turkey in roasting in oven and cook for about 2 hours, or until the internal temperature is 160-165 degrees. Remove from oven, let cool, and shred into long strands.

For the Molasses Vinaigrette

1 shallot, finely chopped
3 garlic cloves, finely chopped
1 teaspoon salt
½ teaspoon black pepper

1 tablespoon molasses
½ cup rice vinegar
2 tablespoons sesame oil
¾ cup peanut oil

COMBINE all ingredients except the oils in a medium bowl. Slowly whisk in the oils.

SESAME CRUSTED AHI TUNA

with Star Anise Basmati Rice, Braised Shiitake Broth,
finished with Wasabi-Ginger Compound Butter

Ingredients

4 6-ounce pieces of Ahi tuna
3 tablespoons white sesame seeds
3 tablespoons black sesame seeds
   Star Anise Basmati Rice (recipe
   follows)

Braised Shiitake Broth (recipe follows)
Wasabi-Ginger Compound Butter
(recipe follows)

Preparation

MIX the white and black sesame seeds together. Coat 1 side of the tuna with the mixture. Sear in a hot skillet to desired temperature. Do not overcook tuna.

TO SERVE, place basmati rice on plate and place tuna on top. Cover with broth, then slice compound butter and place on top of tuna.

Serves 4

For the Star Anise Basmati Rice

2 tablespoons canola oil
½ yellow onion, finely minced
1 stick cinnamon

3 star anise
1 cup basmati rice
3 cups water

IN A heavy-bottomed saucepan sauté onion in oil over medium heat. Add remaining ingredients and reduce heat to low. Simmer, covered, for about 20 minutes, until rice is cooked and water is evaporated. Remove cinnamon and star anise, and keep rice warm.

For Braised Shiitake Broth

½ pound shiitake mushrooms
1 tablespoon sesame oil
3 tablespoons peanut oil
1 shallot, thinly sliced
½ cup sherry

2 tablespoons mirin
2 tablespoons sugar
¼ cup soy sauce
3 cups chicken broth

IN A large skillet, heat oil over medium-high heat and sauté mushrooms until golden brown and a nutty aroma is evident. Add shallot and sauté a few more minutes. Deglaze pan with sherry. Add remaining ingredients and bring to a boil. Cook 10 to 15 minutes

For the Wasabi-Ginger Compound Butter

4 ounces butter, room temperature
1 tablespoon powdered wasabi

1 teaspoon fresh ginger, minced
2 scallions, chopped

BLEND all ingredients until evenly incorporated. Shape mixture into desired shape and chill.

Braised Bison Short Ribs

with Tomato and Fennel, served atop Soft Polenta

Ingredients

4 bison short rib slabs	2 stalks celery, chopped
2 teaspoons salt	4 garlic cloves, minced
1 tablespoon black pepper	1 16-ounce can chopped tomatoes
2 teaspoons cayenne	2 cups red wine
2 teaspoons dried basil	3 cups chicken broth
1 yellow onion, julienned	Soft Polenta (recipe follows)
1 fennel bulb with fronds, chopped	

Preparation

HEAT oven to 450 degrees. Combine salt, pepper, cayenne, and basil and rub onto ribs. Heat oil in heavy-bottomed large casserole dish over medium-high heat. Add ribs and sear on both sides, about 3-4 minutes per side. Remove and set aside.

ADD onion, fennel, celery, and garlic to dish and sauté for about 5 minutes, or until vegetables become soft. Deglaze pan with red wine and reduce for about 5 minutes. Add tomatoes and return ribs to casserole, covering all with chicken broth. Cover and place in 450-degee oven for about 3 hours or until tender. Check casserole after 2 hours and add more liquid if ribs are drying.

TO SERVE, place Soft Polenta on the bottom of large pasta bowls or plates. Place a serving of ribs on top. Ladle sauce over top of ribs and around the polenta.

Serves 4

For the Soft Polenta

½ cup yellow cornmeal	½ cup grated Parmesan
3 cups water	½ teaspoon white pepper
2 tablespoons butter	salt to taste

BRING water to a boil and slowly whisk in cornmeal. Reduce heat to low, cover, and simmer, stirring every 5 minutes. Cook about 20 minutes. Remove from heat and stir in Parmesan, pepper, and salt to taste. Keep warm until ready to serve.

Ferraro's Fine Italian Restaurant

FERRARO'S
FINE ITALIAN

726 N 7th Ave
Bozeman, MT 59715
(406) 587-2555
(406) 582-1651

Open 7 days a week from 5:00 p.m.
Reservations for parties of 5 or
more only

Ferraro's Fine Italian Restaurant

Ralph Ferraro & Mike Hope, Owners
Ralph Ferraro, Executive Chef

R alph Ferraro has been a Bozeman institution since he came here in 1972. He has been in the restaurant business for over 35 years, beginning his culinary experience in Vail, Colorado under a Swiss chef. The rest of his experience, Ralph says, "has been gained in the school of hard knocks".

From 1972 to 1980, Ralph owned and managed 8 restaurants and bars throughout the state of Montana. He started the famous Overland Express in downtown Bozeman in the old Bozeman Hotel. The restaurant specialized in steaks and seafood and featured a rustic western atmosphere. He eventually opened 3 other Overland Express restaurants in Helena, Missoula, and Great Falls. Ralph sold the restaurants in 1981.

In 1978, he purchased the Rocking R Bar, turning it into a Bozeman tradition. Then, in 1988, Ralph purchased the building on North 7th Avenue that was to become Ferraro's. For the first few years, he rented the building as an ice cream parlor. Then, in 1991, he took over the property and opened a casino in the building. In 1995, Ralph opened Ferraro's. The restaurant was accessed by going through the casino, but had its own warm Italian ambience.

The building was completely remodeled in 2003. The casino was closed and Ferraro's Fine Italian Restaurant took over the complete location. Done in a Tuscan style of architecture, the building was opened up to include a glass-walled dining room in the back. The room that served as the original Ferraro's was preserved with its cozy, dark interior and arched windows.

You will find a wide range of Italian entrées featuring the finest meats and seafood accompanied by family style servings of crisp salad with a house vinaigrette and pasta with your choice of sauces. The veal dishes are exceptional. Or, try one of the luscious pasta specialties made with house-made fresh pasta tossed with a variety of fantastic sauces. Ferraro's has a full bar, but specializes in the best of Italian wines. If you are not as familiar with these wines, your waitperson can direct you to the appropriate wine for your tastes and menu choices. Ralph's Italian background and love of all things Italian comes through in the food as well as the congenial atmosphere that you will experience.

Basic Marinara Sauce

This recipe makes a great marinara that can be used in several of the other recipes in this section. It can also be frozen in small portions for future use. If you want to make the sauce a little richer, you can add 2 teaspoons of chicken base or fat after combining all the ingredients.

Ingredients

2 tablespoons olive oil
6 garlic cloves, diced small
1 yellow onion, diced small
2 celery stalks, diced small

1 large carrot, diced small
1 16-ounce can crushed tomatoes in puree

Preparation

IN A 12- to 14-inch sauté pan over medium to high heat, add the olive oil and heat until it almost smokes. Add the diced garlic, onion, celery and carrot, cooking until soft.

PUT the crushed tomatoes into a large pot, and add the mixture from the sauté pan, stirring to combine. Simmer, covered, for 2½ hours.

Yield 2 quarts

Ferraro's, Bozeman

59

BASIC PASTA DOUGH

For making pasta dough at home, I have found that the Atlas Pasta Machine does the best job. You can also roll the dough out by hand, but the pasta machine will save you a lot of time and effort.

Ingredients

4 cups all purpose flour, or less
8 eggs

½ teaspoon extra virgin olive oil

Preparation

PUT 3½ to 4 cups flour in a large mixing bowl, leaving a depression in the center of the flour. Add the eggs and olive oil in the middle of the flour. Using a fork beat together the eggs and oil, and begin to incorporate the flour.

AS THE dough comes together, start kneading it, using the palms of both hands. Knead for about 6 minutes. The dough should be elastic and a little sticky. Wrap the dough in plastic and allow it to rest for 30 minutes at room temperature. Unwrap dough and, using a pasta machine, make noodles as desired.

YOU can also make noodles by hand with the dough. Working in batches, roll out the dough on a flat surface that is lightly dusted with flour. Fold the dough in half and then in half again. Roll the dough out again. Repeat the process several times, until the dough starts to have a silkier feeling. Roll it out the last time to the thickness of the type of pasta that you want, and then cut strips or shapes as desired.

Serves 4 to 6

Bucatini all' Amatriciana

Bucatini is a pasta similar to spaghetti, but with a hole through it resembling a drinking straw.

Ingredients

8 ounces pancetta (can substitute
  regular bacon if necessary)
3 garlic cloves, sliced thin
1 red onion, cut in half and sliced
1½ teaspoons red chili flakes

salt and pepper to taste
16 ounces Marinara Sauce (see recipe
  this section)
1 pound bucatini pasta
  Pecorino Romano, to taste

Preparation

IN A 12 to 14-inch sauté pan, heat the pancetta until it begins to release its fat, and then add garlic, onion, and chili flakes. Sauté until the onion is soft. Season with salt and pepper. Add Marinara Sauce, reduce heat, and simmer for 10 to 15 minutes.

MEANWHILE, in a large pot of boiling salted water, cook the pasta until al dente. Drain and add to the sauce, stirring to coat the pasta.

TO SERVE, place in pasta bowls and sprinkle with Pecorino Romano.

Serves 6 to 8

Wine suggestion: Gaja 1995 Barolo Sperss

LINGUINE CON RED VONGOLE SAUCE
(Red Clam Sauce)

Ingredients

4 teaspoons extra virgin olive oil
2 garlic cloves, diced small
1 teaspoon red chili flakes
6 clams, canned or fresh
¼ cup Marinara Sauce (see recipe in this section)

¼ cup fish stock, or clam juice
8 ounces linguine
   chopped parsley, for garnish

Preparation

IN A 12 to 14-inch sauté pan over medium high heat, add the olive oil and then the garlic and sauté until the garlic is soft. Add the red chili flakes, clams, Marinara Sauce, and fish stock. Simmer for about 10 minutes.

MEANWHILE, add linguini to a large pot of boiling salted water, and cook until al dente. When done, drain linguini and add to clam sauce, stirring to combine.

TO SERVE, place in a pasta bowl and sprinkle with fresh parsley.

Serves 1

Wine suggestion: Poderi Colla 1997 (Piedmont Nebbiolo grape)

NAPOLITANA
Fettuccine in the Style of Naples

Ingredients

¼ cup extra virgin olive oil
1 teaspoon fresh garlic, minced
5 large shrimp
¼ cup fish stock

½ cup Marinara Sauce (see recipe in this section)
8 ounces cooked fettuccine noodles
1 pinch fresh oregano

Preparation

IN A 12 to 14-inch sauté pan, heat the olive oil and add the garlic, sautéing until soft. Add shrimp and sauté for about 1 minute. Add the fish stock and sauté for 3 to 4 minutes. Add marinara sauce and simmer for 10 minutes. Add the cooked fettuccine, stirring to coat the pasta. Finish with a pinch of oregano and serve immediately.

Serves 1

Wine suggestion: 1999 Castello D'Quercito – a Tuscany Cabernet Sauvignon

The patio at Ferraro's.

POLLO AL LA ROMANA

Ingredients

¼ cup extra virgin olive oil
2 ounces pancetta, chopped fine
2 cloves garlic, chopped fine
4 boneless, skinless chicken breasts
½ cup Frascatti, or other dry white wine
1 16-ounce can crushed tomatoes and
   juice

2 green bell peppers, seeded and cut into
   strips
2 red bell peppers, seeded and cut into
   strips
   salt and pepper to taste

Preparation

IN A 12- to 14-inch sauté pan, heat the olive oil over medium heat. Add the pancetta and cook slowly to render out much of the fat. Remove all but 4 tablespoons of the fat-oil mixture from the pan. Add the garlic and chicken, cooking until the chicken begins to change color and the garlic browns. Add the wine and cook 5 minutes. Add the tomatoes and peppers, season with salt and pepper to taste.

SIMMER, uncovered, for 15 minutes, or until chicken is cooked through.

Serves 4

Wine suggestion: Guado al Tasso 1999 Antinori

Gallatin River Lodge

GALLATIN RIVER LODGE

Established 1999

9105 Thorpe Road
One mile west of State Route 85
(off Jackrabbit Lane)
Bozeman, MT 59718
www.grlodge.com

Open year-round for lodging
or for dinner only
406-388-0148
Bar opens at 4:30 pm
Dinner service 5:30-9:30 nightly

Gallatin River Lodge

Steve & Christy Gamble, Owners
Mitchell Kayser, Chef

Gallatin River Lodge, just minutes from Bozeman and Yellowstone National Park, is a year-round full-service fly-fishing lodge. The finest, most diverse fly fishing in the world is found just out the door on the Gallatin, Yellowstone, and Madison Rivers and private nearby streams.

The menu reflects influences from many different cuisines, including Baked Brie, Sweet Cajun Shrimp, and Bison New York Strip. Local favorites include lamb chops and steelhead trout. House-baked breads accompany each meal, and to finish things off, choose from a creative selection of desserts to tempt your sweet tooth.

"The Gallatin River Grill" is open seven nights a week to the general public as well as guests of the lodge. Chef Mitchell Kayser and Sous Chef Kris Kahao offer a new menu each week that has given the grill an exceptional reputation for dining. Entrées include certified Angus beef, buffalo, duck, pheasant, pork, lamb, and fish prepared in the style of creative Northwest American cuisine. Accorded the Wine Spectator Award of Excellence, the restaurant offers a nice selection of fine wines as well as a top-shelf bar to enhance your dining.

The 50-seat dining room with fir floors, oak furnishings, and a turn-of-the-century oak back bar offer a comfortable environment to enjoy a meal or a drink from the full-service bar. You can watch white-tailed deer graze by the trout pond or enjoy the spectacular views of the Spanish Peaks and Bridger Mountains while the dining room staff takes care of your every need.

Year-round service includes fine dining, conference, wedding, and catering services, and nightly bed and breakfast accommodations. Six suites are perfect for couples or anglers and contain rustic but elegant decor, fireplaces, Jacuzzi tubs, and spectacular views of the mountains and river habitat. A complete fly-fishing guide service is also available.

Award of Excellence

Gallatin River Lodge, Bozeman

Tomato & Parmesan Soup

Ingredients

1 tablespoon olive oil
1 cup celery, small dice
2 cups onion, small dice
1 shallot, small dice
1 cup carrot, small dice
2 tablespoons red wine
2 garlic cloves, rough chopped

3 cups canned diced tomatoes
1 teaspoon dry thyme
6 cups chicken broth
½ cup heavy cream
1 cup freshly grated Parmesan cheese, divided

Preparation

OVER high heat in a large pot, add olive oil and sauté the celery, onion, shallot, and carrot until caramelized. Add the wine to deglaze the pot. Now add the garlic, tomato, thyme and chicken broth, stirring to combine. Bring the mixture to a boil and turn down the heat to a simmer; let the mixture simmer for 20 minutes. Add the heavy cream and ½ cup of the Parmesan cheese. Bring back to a simmer and then remove the pot from the heat. Let the mixture cool for 15 minutes.

WITH a hand blender or a regular blender, blend to a liquid consistency and adjust the flavor with salt and pepper. Caution: if using a glass blender, make sure to warm it up with hot water so it is tempered and won't break. Always use a towel on top of a blender when pureeing hot liquids.

TO SERVE, pour into individual soup bowls and garnish with the remaining Parmesan.

Serves 6

BBQ Duck Breast

with Raspberry BBQ Sauce and Creamy White Cheddar Polenta

Ingredients

4 duck breasts
salt and pepper to taste
Raspberry BBQ Sauce (recipe follows)

Creamy Polenta with White Cheddar
(recipe follows)

Preparation

WITH a sharp knife, score the fat on each breast. Place a breast in a plastic sandwich bag and lightly pound with a mallet. Repeat with the other 3 breasts. This will allow a larger surface and an even cooking area. Dust each breast with salt and pepper.

OVER a warm grill, place the breasts fat side down. Flip the breasts over after a few minutes and continue cooking until desired doneness. Do not overcook. Duck breast is best when it is rare to medium rare. Just before the duck is finished, you can reheat the polenta pieces on the grill.

TO SERVE, place 1 breast on each plate and drizzle Raspberry BBQ Sauce over and around the breast. Place a piece of the Creamy Polenta to the side.

Serves 4

For the Raspberry BBQ Sauce

2 yellow onions, rough chopped
2 garlic cloves, minced
½ cup red wine
½ cup brewed coffee
⅓ cup Worcestershire sauce
1 cup ketchup
1 cup orange juice
2 tablespoons lemon juice
1 dash Tabasco
1 cup water

2 tablespoons molasses
1 small can tomato paste
1 tablespoon ground mustard seed
1 tablespoon Colman's dry mustard
2 tablespoons brown sugar
1 tablespoon sugar
1 teaspoon cayenne pepper
1 teaspoon chili powder
2½ cups frozen raspberries
salt and pepper to taste

Preparation

IN A large saucepan, sweat the onion and garlic with a little oil until the onion begins to turn clear. Add the wine, stir, and simmer until the liquid is absorbed. Now add all the other liquids, including the molasses and tomato paste, stirring to combine. Then add the dry ingredients, again stirring to combine. Stir in the raspberries. Let the mixture simmer for about an hour, and then remove from heat and let the sauce cool. Purée the cooled mixture in a blender and adjust the flavor with salt and pepper. For a smoother sauce, you may want to strain it to remove the raspberry seeds.

Yield approximately 2 to 3 cups

For the Creamy Polenta with White Cheddar

1 medium onion, finely chopped
1 ounce white wine
2 cups water
2½ cups chicken broth
1½ cups polenta
7 garlic cloves, minced

1 red bell pepper, finely chopped
1 pinch parsley, chopped
2 ounces white cheddar, cut in small cubes
1 ounce Parmesan cheese, grated

OVER medium heat in a large pan, brown the onion in a small amount of oil. Add the wine and cook down until most of the liquid is gone. Now add the water and the stock, bringing the mixture to a boil. Add the polenta, stirring, and let it start to cook. Once the mixture starts to thicken, add the rest of the ingredients, stirring to combine. Adjust the flavor with salt and pepper. When the polenta has thickened, remove it from the heat and pour it onto a sheet pan to cool. Once it is cool, cut shapes with a large cookie cutter.

Serves 4

Pierpont ("Jack") Morgan II hunting party. (1880)

John Bozeman's Bistro

Established in 1983

125 West Main
Bozeman, MT 59715
Historic downtown Bozeman
406–587–4100
www.johnbozemansbistro.com

Reservations recommended
Lunch, 11:30 am to 2:30 pm
Dinner, 5:00 to 9:30 pm
Closed Sundays and Mondays

The chefs at John Bozeman's Bistro.

John Bozeman's Bistro

Tyler and Carla Hill, Owners
Perry Wenzel, Chef

O
n July 7, 1864, Daniel E. Rouse and William J. Beall drafted plans for the townsite of Bozeman, named for John Bozeman who first came to Montana in search of gold. When that didn't pan out, John decided to help the miners. In 1863, he and John Jacobs blazed the Bozeman Trail, a cutoff route from the Oregon Trail, and guided miners to Virginia City through the Gallatin Valley.

One of the restaurants inspired by this city's history is John Bozeman's Bistro, an original fine-dining experience with Montana hospitality in its one-of-a-kind setting. The imaginative "World Cuisine," fine wines, quality brews, and great service are enhanced by the unique design of the renovated 1905 downtown building. The façade of the building is a replica of the way things were in the early 1900s. Your feet will cross a floor of multicolored slate from Florence, Italy as you enter. On the west side of the restaurant are the restored 1930s booths with glass partitions to ensure your dining privacy. The original art deco lights over the granite bar hang from the 90-year-old restored ceiling. For over 20 years, the Bistro has been known as a local favorite for its creative treatment of the freshest ingredients and its international flair with a multi-dimensional flavor.

SUMMER PICNIC BREAD SALAD

Ingredients

4 cups dried rustic or artisan bread (no
    Wonder bread please!)
1 cup ripe tomato, diced
½ cup red bell pepper, diced
1 cup English cucumber, diced
½ cup green olives, sliced
½ cup red onion, sliced
½ cup fresh basil, chopped
1 cup canned Italian white beans

½ cup Italian parsley, chopped
1 cup aged Provolone cheese, cubed
¾ cup red wine vinegar
½ cup extra virgin olive oil
1 teaspoon Dijon style mustard
½ teaspoon dried oregano
¼ teaspoon sugar
    salt and freshly ground pepper to taste

Preparation

IN A large bowl, mix together the ingredients from the bread cubes to the Provolone cheese. In a small bowl or pitcher, combine the vinegar, oil, mustard, oregano, and sugar. Adjust seasonings to taste with salt and pepper.

ADD the dressing to the salad, tossing gently to coat the vegetables. Place the salad in the refrigerator for 2 hours before serving.

Serves 6 to 8

The inviting interior of the present-day Bistro.

BRAISED ITALIAN RADICCHIO

Ingredients

1 cup prosciutto ham, shredded	½ teaspoon roasted fennel seed
½ cup Italian parsley, chopped	2 heads radicchio, cut in small wedges
½ Italian Parmigiano cheese, shredded	⅓ cup white wine
2 tablespoons olive oil	2 tablespoons vegetable or chicken stock
1 cup onion, chopped	lemon juice
1 teaspoon fresh garlic, minced	freshly ground black pepper

Preparation

IN A bowl, mix together the prosciutto ham, parsley and cheese. Set aside.

SAUTÉ the onion, garlic and fennel seed in the olive oil for 3 to 5 minutes. Add radicchio and continue sautéing on high for another 2 to 3 minutes. Add wine and stock; cover and steam until the leaves become slightly tender.

ADD the radicchio mix to the bowl containing the prosciutto mixture, tossing to combine. Season to taste with lemon juice and freshly ground black pepper. Serve immediately.

Serves 4

You can expect out-of-the-ordinary lunches at the Bistro.

Santa Fe Venison Cassoulet

Ingredients

2 pounds lean stew meat (antelope, deer, elk), cut in 1-inch cubes
2 tablespoons canned puréed chipotles
3 teaspoons Mexi Spice (recipe follows)
2 tablespoons olive oil
2 tablespoons flour
⅓ cup olive oil
1 tablespoon garlic, minced
2 cups onion, chopped
1 cup celery, chopped
2 cups pasilla or bell peppers, chopped
1 cup dark beer
1 cup tomato, chopped
1 cup cilantro, chopped
1 16-ounce can diced green chilies
4 cups beef broth
canned white beans (optional)
tomatoes, chopped for garnish
cilantro, chopped for garnish
salt and pepper to taste

Preparation

IN A large bowl, hand blend the venison cubes with the puréed chipotle, Mexi Spice, and 2 tablespoons olive oil. Add flour to coat evenly.

HEAT a large braising pan, add ⅓ cup olive oil and brown the venison for about 5 minutes. Add the garlic, onion, celery and peppers. Sweat the vegetables until they start to soften. Add the beer, tomato, cilantro, and green chilies. Stir in the beef broth.

SIMMER 2 hours until the meat is tender. Add the canned white beans if you prefer. Finish with more chopped cilantro and chopped tomatoes, and season to taste with salt and pepper.

THE cassoulet can be served over polenta, rice, mashed potatoes, toast, or pasta.

Serves 6 to 8

For the Mexi Spice

MIX together equal parts of

ground cumin
ground coriander
ground dry mustard
granulated garlic

chili powder
Kosher salt
oregano
freshly ground black pepper

ANY extra spice can be kept in a glass jar with a tightly sealed lid for future use.

Fishing on the Gallatin River at the turn of the century was not so different from today. One still must keep a watchful eye for the occasional grizzly.

320
Guest
Ranch

205 Buffalo Horn Creek
Highway 191, Mile Marker 36,
Big Sky, MT 59716
1-800-243-0320 or 406-995-4283
www.320ranch.com

Reservations recommended
Open seasonally
Hours 5:30 to 9:00 pm

320 Guest Ranch

David Brask, Owner
Pat Sage, General Manager
Jeff Tappero, Chef

Deep in the heart of the Gallatin National Forest, the 320 Guest Ranch is located just minutes from Yellowstone National Park and Big Sky Ski Resort, with two miles of the renowned Gallatin River running through the property.

The 320 Guest Ranch and Resort offers a large variety of activities during the winter and summer months. In winter, the 320 Ranch features starlit sleigh rides to the Mountain Man Campsite, snowmobile excursions into Yellowstone Park, and Montana meals in the cozy restaurant complete with rock fireplace. In addition, the surrounding area offers some of the best backcountry snowmobiling and skiing—downhill, cross-country, and backcountry—to be found anywhere in the Rockies. For those interested in Yellowstone Park, the 320 is just 36 miles away, and snowmobile or snow coach trips can be arranged. Hike on snowshoes through deep powder for a truly exhilarating workout. Relax as a team of sled dogs pulls you along, yipping in excitement.

The 320 Ranch is also located near some of the best hunting in the world—from big game like elk, moose, and deer to ducks and grouse. They offer special hunting-season rates you won't find anywhere else.

The ranch comes alive in the summer with lots of fun outdoor activities and a true Western experience. Take a trail ride through the Gallatin National Forest with the ranch's wranglers, hike forest trails, fish in blue-ribbon trout streams, or sit on your front porch and enjoy the breathtaking scenery. Montana summers provide many adventures: historic ghost towns to be explored, whitewater rafting, mountain biking tours, rock climbing, tours of Yellowstone Park or a guided hike—the list of activities seems endless.

The 320 Guest Ranch launched into a stunning historical journey in the year 1898 when Sam Wilson homesteaded 160 acres along the Gallatin River. In 1900, Sam's father, Clinton, claimed an adjoining 160 acres and they combined the two properties and named the consolidated parcel the Buffalo Horn Resort. The original homestead cabin is still an important part of the 320 Guest Ranch and has been preserved as a part of the restaurant.

A bird's eye view of the 320 Ranch in Gallatin Canyon.

Dr. Caroline McGill

In 1904 employees of the Cooper Tie Logging Company constructed several cabins on the ranch in exchange for lodging. They worked the nearby Taylor Fork drainage, preparing timber for use as railroad ties. When the logging company went out of business in 1906, the Eldridge Post Office building was moved to the ranch and continued operating from there until it closed in 1938.

On January 16, 1936, Dr. Caroline McGill, a woman far ahead of her time, purchased the ranch from Mrs. Wilson. Montana's first woman doctor and first pathologist, Dr. McGill was an avid hunter and fisher. She believed that enjoying the outdoors was beneficial and bought the ranch as a place for her patients and friends to come to relax.

In 1938, Dr. McGill purchased a Cadillac engine in Idaho Falls that a friend, Jim Flint, installed to generate power. The ranch had power 10 years before power lines came into Gallatin Canyon.

The ranch crew decided to build Dr. McGill a cabin closer to the office due to her advancing age. Finished on Christmas, it is known as the Christmas Cabin. She passed away in 1959. In her will, she gave the Goodrich family the option to purchase the 320 Guest Ranch. The family did buy the ranch and continued to run it as a guest ranch until 1987 when the current owner, Dave Brask, purchased it.

Under the ownership of Mr. Brask, the 320 Guest Ranch has grown from a capacity of 20 guests to well over 200. In the process, Mr. Brask has preserved all of the buildings that could be saved. The original homestead cabin is now a part of the 320 Steakhouse, containing antiques that Dave has purchased in his travels. He had Dr. McGill's original ranch house moved from the middle of the front pasture to a more peaceful setting near Buffalo Horn Creek.

The Christmas Cabin still remains and is occupied by 320 Ranch staff. Very few of the original buildings could be saved, but Dave has captured the feel of Montana with all of the new cabins and homes built of logs. Dave Brask enjoys the outdoors and believes in keeping the 320 Guest Ranch diverse in its operation and preserving the authenticity of the ranch atmosphere.

Dinnertime at the 320 Ranch in the 1940's.

BACON-WRAPPED PHEASANT
with Merlot Honey Butter

Ingredients

3 2-pound pheasants, cut in quarters
24 strips bacon

salt and pepper to taste
Merlot Honey Butter (recipe follows)

Preparation

HEAT oven to 300 degrees. Season pheasant quarters and wrap each piece with 2 strips of bacon. Place bacon-wrapped pheasant on a sheet pan and roast in oven for 15-20 minutes.

TO SERVE, place a breast and leg piece on each serving plate and spoon sauce over all.

Serves 6

For the Merlot Honey Butter

½ bottle merlot wine
1 medium shallot, finely diced
2 garlic cloves, finely diced

2 teaspoons honey
1 tablespoon butter

PLACE shallots, garlic, and wine in a saucepan. Over low heat, reduce by three-fourths. Strain mixture and discard garlic and shallots. Return to a simmer and add honey. Slowly add butter, stirring constantly. Keep warm until ready to serve.

A couple enjoys an intimate evening at the 320 Ranch.

WAPITI PICATA

Ingredients

3 2-ounce wapiti (elk) tenderloin
   medallions
¼ cup flour
1 teaspoon shallots, finely diced

1 tablespoon capers, with juice
½ lemon
¼ cup heavy cream
   salt and pepper to taste

SEASON the flour to taste. Lightly coat the elk with flour. Preheat the oil in a sauté pan over medium heat. Lightly sear each side of the elk, approximately 2 minutes. Add the shallots and capers with juice. Slice one slice of lemon and set aside for garnish. Squeeze the juice from the remaining lemon and add to the pan. Reduce the heat to simmer and add the cream. Reduce by one half and serve immediately. Butterfly the lemon slice for garnish.

Serves 1

CAST-IRON TROUT
with Fresh Herbs and Lemon

Ingredients

½ cup flour
1 8-ounce trout butterflied with bones
   removed
½ lemon
1 teaspoon fresh thyme, finely chopped

1 teaspoon fresh rosemary, finely
   chopped
1 tablespoon butter
   salt and pepper to taste

PREHEAT a cast-iron skillet over medium heat. Season the flour with salt and pepper. Lightly flour the trout. Add the butter to the skillet. Place the trout in the skillet skin side up. Cook until lightly browned and turn over. Slice a piece of lemon for garnish. Take a pinch of herbs and sprinkle over the trout. Squeeze the rest of the lemon juice over the trout, garnish and serve.

Serves 1

320 Berry Cobbler

Ingredients

4 cups Bisquick
1 cup milk
¼ cup rum
½ cup powdered sugar

7 cups fresh or frozen berries
¾ cup granulated sugar
cornstarch (as needed)

HEAT oven to 350 degrees.

MIX Bisquick, milk, rum, and powdered sugar. Put in cast-iron pot. Bake until toothpick comes out dry. Let cool. Tip pot upside down and let breading fall out. Replace with berries and granulated sugar. Bring to a boil and add cornstarch until thick.

DROP breading on top and sprinkle with additional powdered sugar.

Serves 8-10

Lu Bar cook making bread. (August 1904)

Buck's T-4 Lodge

U.S. Highway 191, (one mile south
of the Big Sky spur road)
Big Sky, MT 59716
1-800-822-4484 or 406-995-4111
info@buckst4.com

www.buckst4.com
Open seasonally winter and summer
Dining 7 days/week 6:00 to 9:30 pm
Lodging available

Buck's T-4 in 1972.

Buck's T-4 Lodge
A Big Sky Tradition

Mike Scholz, Owner
David O'Conner, General Manager
Scott Peterson, Chef

Buck's T-4 began as a hunting lodge in 1946, eventually growing into one of southwest Montana's favorite road-houses. Buck and Helen Knight opened the business with a philosophy of home-cooked food and genuine, friendly service. Buck's "Lazy T-4" brand became synonymous with friends, food, and fun in Gallatin Canyon. Mike Scholz purchased the lodge from the Knights in 1972, and has kept that philosophy interwoven in his business today.

The original bar that Buck Knight built in 1952 from local lodgepole pine is the oldest part of the complex and is still in use today, with many of Helen's special touches. There is even a large game room with video games and pool tables.

The adjoining bar was constructed in 1972 using two adjacent cabins, turning each 90 degrees and framing them in together. The construction was accomplished by Buck and a few friends using wood from the property. The tongue-and-groove ceiling, handmade bar, and unpeeled log accents exemplify the style and craftsmanship of mid-century rural Montana. Great care has been taken to preserve the original construction and feel of the building.

A new dining room adjacent to the original bar was also built in 1972, as well as a large dance hall, which soon became known as one of Montana's raucous and rowdy roadhouses. Large dances were held most weekends in the mid to late seventies, often featuring Montana's Mission Mountain Wood Band. In subsequent years, a lounge, three private dining rooms and a large dining room addition, display wine cellar, and

Buck's T-4 today.

state-of-the-art kitchen were added. Later, a more casual restaurant opened, featuring pizza and hamburgers with pool tables and video games. While the dance hall now holds more weddings than wildness, and the restaurant sees more culinarians than cowboys, Buck's T-4 still has echoes of its roadhouse past.

Mike believes in providing the best possible cuisine and service for guests, while retaining the original Montana ambiance that started with the Knights. He feels that culinary excellence and pretension do not necessarily go hand-in-hand.

The combination of Mike's unwavering dedication to providing superior dining for his guests and the chef's culinary artistry has created a top-notch experience. Their approach is the application of classical techniques to traditional local ingredients. Some of the game meats he has featured include South Dakota bison, South Texas antelope, New Zealand red deer, North American wapiti (elk) and Alaskan caribou. In 1999, Buck's T-4 was invited to participate at the prestigious James Beard Foundation in New York. Buck's has the honor of being the first restaurant from Montana to be invited. While the Buck's T-4 menu focuses on wild game, his guests also enjoy the hand-cut steaks, seafood, and other unique creations.

Located in the shadow of Lone Peak and the Big Sky Ski and Summer Resort, and but a stone's throw from Yellowstone National Park, the Big Sky community is swiftly becoming one of the most popular vacation destinations in Montana. Visitors enjoy all the excitement the Rocky Mountains have to offer, including whitewater rafting, hiking, horseback riding, and fly fishing in the renowned blue-ribbon waters of the Gallatin River. Big Sky also offers world-class skiing in the winter, having grown to be the fourth largest ski area in the United States.

 Award of Excellence

The wine room at Buck's T-4.

WILD GAME MEATLOAF

Ingredients

1 cup red onion, fine diced
1 cup green onion, fine diced
½ cup carrot, fine diced
⅓ cup celery stalk, fine diced
⅓ cup green bell pepper, fine diced
⅓ cup red bell pepper, fine diced
1 tablespoon peeled clove garlic, finely chopped
1 tablespoon kosher salt
1½ teaspoons freshly-ground black peppercorn

1 teaspoon white ground pepper
½ teaspoon cayenne pepper
1½ teaspoons ground cumin
1 teaspoon ground nutmeg
3 pounds wild game trim, ground
1 pound bulk pork sausage
⅓ cup ketchup
1 cup crouton crumbs
2 tablespoons butter
4 large eggs
3 cups half-and-half

Preparation

HEAT oven to 375 degrees.

SAUTÉ vegetables and garlic in butter until al dente. Cool mixture until chilled.

PLACE ground game trim in mixer with pork sausage, cooled vegetables, spices, ketchup, and crouton crumbs. Place dough hook on mixer and mix on low speed. Add eggs, one at a time. If no mixer is available, knead by hand until fully incorporated. Add half-and-half to meat mixture.

PLACE mixture into two bread pans, making sure bottom is free of any air pockets and top is smooth and domed in the center, then individually wrap each meatloaf with foil.

BAKE at 375 degrees in a water bath until internal temperature of meatloaf reaches 155 degrees.

REMOVE meatloaf from water bath, unwrap and pour off excess grease. Remove from bread pans, slice, and serve with Marinated Tomato & Roasted Garlic Sauce (recipe follows).

Makes two loaves

Marinated Tomato & Roasted Garlic Sauce

Ingredients

1¼ pounds Roma tomatoes, medium dice
3 ounces whole-peeled garlic cloves (about 18 cloves)
¼ cup olive oil
¼ ounce fresh basil chiffonade (shredded)

2 shallots, finely diced
3 ounces tomato paste
1 ounce balsamic vinegar
salt and pepper to taste

Preparation

COMBINE garlic cloves and olive oil in saucepan and simmer on low until garlic is soft, but do not allow garlic to brown, as it will become bitter. Set aside.

COMBINE tomatoes, shallots, basil, tomato paste, and balsamic vinegar. Pour warm softened garlic and olive oil over tomato mixture. Stir to combine. Season with salt and pepper. Refrigerate.

BRING to room temperature before serving or warm in a microwave.

Smoked Corn Relish

Ingredients

12 ears of smoked corn
1 green pepper, diced
1 medium onion, diced
4 Roma tomatoes, diced
1 cup granulated sugar (reduce sugar to ½ cup if grilling)

1-1¼ cups cider vinegar
1 teaspoon turmeric
1 teaspoon yellow mustard seed
salt and pepper to taste

Preparation

SMOKE or grill corn on gas or charcoal barbecue grill, brushing with maple syrup and grilling on all sides until kernels are tender.

CUT corn kernels from cobs and combine all ingredients and simmer half an hour. Adjust to desired consistency with cornstarch.

WILD GAME PATÉ

Ingredients

1¼ cup whole pistachios	¾ pound pork fat
½ pound peeled shallots, chopped	1 tablespoon kosher salt
¾ tablespoons butter, melted	1 tablespoon ground black pepper
½ tablespoon fresh sage	½ quart heavy whipping cream
1 tablespoon fresh thyme	4 large eggs
5 pounds wild game trim (can use any	¾ cup brandy
red game meat)	thin-sliced pancetta or prosciutto
1¼ pound wild boar bacon	

Preparation

HEAT oven to 350 degrees.

ROAST pistachios in oven until slightly browned, then cool. Saute shallots in butter with sage and thyme over medium heat and cool.

DOUBLE grind wild game trim, boar bacon, and pork fat, first with ½-inch plate, then with ¼-inch plate. Slightly frozen meat works best. Add meat, shallots, pistachios, and remaining ingredients to mixer and mix with paddle. If no mixer is available, knead mixture with hands until fully incorporated. Allow mixture to rest in refrigerator overnight so flavors can mellow and incorporate.

The Following Day

LINE loaf pans with pancetta or prosciutto. Fill pans with raw paté mixture and top with more pancetta. Wrap each loaf pan in aluminum foil. Fill a large roasting pan half full of water. Place loaf pans in this water bath and bake at 350 degrees for about 1½ hours, or until internal temperature reaches 145 degrees and juices are running clear. Remove paté from oven.

APPLY weight to each paté by placing an empty loaf pan on each, then a sheet pan over both and about 60 pounds of weight on the sheet pan. Let cool overnight.

TO SERVE, slice into wedges and serve with sourdough bread, lingonberry sauce, huckleberry mustard, and stone-ground mustard.

Makes 2 loaves

Lone Mountain Ranch

Lone Mountain Ranch

Discovery is in our nature.

Established 1915

Lone Mtn. Ranch Access Rd.,
Spur 64 west off Hwy. 191
Big Sky, MT 59716
406-995-2782
Reservations, 1-800-514-4644
www.lmranch.com

Breakfast, 7:00 to 9:00 a.m.
Lunch, 11:30 a.m. – 1:30 p.m. (summer)
12:00 – 2:00 p.m. (winter)
Dinner, seating starts at 5:30 p.m.
Open seasonally December to April and
June to October 15

Dining Lodge.

Lone Mountain Ranch

Bob & Vivian Schaap, Owners
Ian Troxler, Chef

Lone Mountain Ranch is rich in the history of Montana. First homesteaded in 1915 as a working cattle and hay ranch, it was purchased in 1926 by Fred Butler, a Chicago paper mill tycoon who built some of the guest cabins still in use. The B-K, as the ranch was called then, was a showplace for the owner's extensive Native American artifact collection. Through the years, the ranch was a logging camp, a boy's ranch, and finally a guest ranch. Bob and Vivian Schaap have owned it since the spring of 1977, hosting guests from all over the world.

The current dining lodge, with its massive stone fireplace, was completed in 1989. The huge chandeliers are made from antlers naturally dropped each winter by bull elk. The Native American artifacts that adorn the walls are from the original B-K collection. In the charming saloon, there is a copper bar and fireplace, a naturally formed curved log that caps the bar, and a huge bull moose watching over everyone.

The Lone Mountain Ranch Dining Room is a wonderfully informal and comfortable non-smoking room. The food has received accolades from guests and has been enthusiastically reviewed in many national publications such as Town and Country, Travel and Leisure, The New York Times, and The Los Angeles Times.

One winter night weekly the ranch guests are transported via horse-drawn sleigh to the remote North Fork cabin for a very special dinner cooked on an old fashioned wood-fired cook stove.

A prime rib dinner is served family-style in a room illuminated by kerosene lanterns. Guitar music and songs round out an evening reminiscent of times long ago.

Lone Mountain dining is best described as creative American regional cuisine. Menus may include venison, lamb, bison, salmon, and duck as well as prime rib, ribeye steaks, pasta specials, poultry, and fresh fish flown in daily.

Hosts Kelly and Yancy Arterburn.

Manhattan Montana Roasted Butterball Potatoes

Here in Montana we raise some of the best potatoes in the country. That state to the southwest of us may be "famous" but our spuds are the best! Spring Creek Farms raises several varieties of potatoes on their family farm in Manhattan, Montana.

Ingredients

- 2 pounds Spring Creek Farms brand German butterball potatoes
- 2 tablespoons chopped fresh herbs (parsley, thyme, sage, rosemary)
- 1 teaspoon smoked Spanish paprika (pimenton)

- ¼ teaspoon Sambal brand chile paste
- 1 tablespoon Montola brand safflower oil

  salt and pepper to taste

Preparation

HEAT oven to 400 degrees. Wash the potatoes and cut them in half so that all the halves are about the same thickness. Put them into a large mixing bowl. Add all of the seasonings and oil to the potatoes and toss until the potatoes are evenly covered with herbs and seasonings.

PLACE each potato cut side down on a flat cookie sheet. Roast the potatoes in a 400° oven until the flesh is soft and the cut side is brown and crispy. Serve hot.

Serves 4 to 6

Interior of dining lodge where guests gather for meals.

BIG SKY NATURAL BEEF POT ROAST

Big Sky Natural Beef raises Scottish highland cattle at two ranches here in Montana. I tell our guests here at Lone Mountain Ranch that Wally Congdon and Skip Hougland raise our beef the way you would raise it for your own family: on beautiful Montana pasture with no hormones or antibiotics.

Purchase a Big Sky Natural Beef (or other Montana raised grass fed beef) boned and tied chuck roast from your favorite natural foods market. The chuck is the perfect cut for pot roast because of its excellent flavor. The long slow cooking process will turn an otherwise under-appreciated cut of meat into a succulent and tender feast.

Ingredients

1 4-6 pound boneless chuck roast	1 carrot, coarsely chopped
1 tablespoon oil for browning	1 celery stalk, coarsely chopped
1 bottle (750 ml) red wine (inexpensive but palatable)	2 cloves garlic, peeled and left whole
	2 tablespoons butter
1 bay leaf	2 tablespoons all purpose flour
1 sprig parsley	1 tablespoon red wine vinegar
1 sprig thyme	2 cups beef stock
1 sprig rosemary	salt and pepper to taste
1 large yellow onion, coarsely chopped	parchment paper

Preparation

HEAT the oven to 300 degrees. Season the roast well with salt and pepper. Next put a little of the oil in a large cast iron Dutch oven or heavy-bottom roasting pan. The pan you choose should be able to go from the stove to the oven and be deep enough to contain the roast and all liquid but not so big that the liquid does not cover the meat. Put the pan on the stove and heat on a medium high burner. Put the roast in the hot pan and brown on all sides to a deep dark brown color. Remove the meat and set aside. Pour a splash of the red wine into the still-hot pan and use a sturdy wooden spoon to help dissolve the pan drippings. Save the drippings with the roast.

TAKE all the herbs and tie them together in a piece of cheesecloth and set aside. Add a little more oil to the pan and put the chopped onion, carrot, celery and the whole garlic cloves into the pan. Sauté the vegetables until they just start to get a little bit of color. Add the butter and flour to the vegetables. Stir constantly until the flour and butter have combined to form a paste on the vegetables; continue stirring for a few more minutes (being careful not to brown the flour). Add the wine, vinegar, beef stock, herbs and garlic to the pot and bring to a simmer. When the liquids are simmering add the meat back into the pot and bring everything back up to a simmer.

PUT a piece of parchment paper cut to the shape of your pan directly on the surface of the liquid. Cover the pan tightly with aluminum foil to create a seal. Place in a 300° oven and cook for 3 hours.

AFTER the meat has cooked, remove it from the pan and keep it warm by wrapping tightly with plastic wrap and placing it in a warm spot. Pour the cooking liquid through a fine mesh strainer into a saucepan. Discard the veggies and herbs at this point. The liquid should be velvety smooth and just a little thinner than gravy. Bring it back to a boil and adjust the seasoning with salt and pepper to your taste. Skim off any separated fat or foam that rises.

SLICE the roast and serve it with the sauce, roasted potatoes and vegetables, and a glass of red wine.

Serves 6 to 8

Cross-country skiing is a 25-year tradition at Lone Mountain Ranch.

ROAST PORK LOIN WITH ONION MARMALADE

We like to support Montana pasture-raised meats. See the Culinary Sources Index for some suppliers you might want to try.

Ingredients

- 3 pounds Montana pasture-raised center-cut pork loin
  Montola brand safflower oil
- 2 sprigs fresh rosemary, chopped

- salt and pepper to taste
- 3 carrots, rough-cut (optional)
- 2 onions, rough-cut (optional)
  Onion Marmalade (recipe follows)

Preparation

Heat oven to 425 degrees. Season the roast with salt and pepper. Lightly coat it with oil and brown it on all sides on a very hot grill or skillet. Rub the roast with rosemary and place on a roasting rack or on top of some rough-cut carrots and onions. Roast in a 425° oven until internal temperature reaches 145° (about 45 minutes to 1 hour). Remove from oven and let rest in a warm place for 15 minutes before slicing.

For the Onion Marmalade

- ⅔ cup red wine vinegar
- ½ cup honey
- 2 large red onions, small dice

- 2 teaspoons coriander seeds, cracked
- 1 tablespoon pink peppercorns, cracked

PUT the vinegar and honey in a heavy bottomed stainless steel saucepan on medium heat. Reduce by three quarters. Add the chopped onions and cracked coriander. (Coriander may be cracked using a mortar and pestle or in the bottom of a heavy skillet with a mallet.) Cook the onions stirring frequently until they are translucent and a consistency similar to jam. Add the pink peppercorns and remove from heat.

COOL the marmalade to room temperature and spoon over the sliced pork loin.

Serves 6

Wine suggestion: A crisp white wine such as Trimbach pinot gris would pair well with this dish.

The Timbers
at Moonlight Lodge

1020 Highway 64
Big Sky, MT 59716
406-995-7777
www.moonlightbasin.com
Open seasonally,
Thanksgiving to April
Mid-June to end of September

Lunch, 11:30 am to 2:30 pm
Dinner, 5:30 to 9:30 pm
(Closed Mondays and Tuesdays in
summer)

The Timbers at Moonlight Lodge

Quinn & Emily Johnson and Monte &
Nancy Johnson, Owners
Scott Mechura, Executive Chef

Located in the breathtaking Moonlight Lodge at Moonlight Basin Ranch, The Timbers Restaurant and Bar offer a unique dining experience in a spectacular setting. The lodge and ranch are just southwest of the Big Sky Resort in the Jack Creek Drainage. The ranch is a luxury mountain community that offers an abundance of outdoor recreation.

Moonlight Lodge's Great Room showcases a spectacular fireplace, elegant furnishings, and breathtaking views of Lone Mountain, all located at 8,000 feet above sea level. The Timbers Bar and Lounge offers a cozy place to relax after a long day on the slopes or the trout streams. Choose from over 40 varieties of Montana micros, domestic, and imported beers, along with the restaurant's expansive wine list, and a full selection of spirits. The Timbers Restaurant boasts a massive stone fireplace and a beautiful wood-beamed ceiling, as well as a sweeping outdoor deck for dining.

Executive Chef Scott Machura offers hearty mountain cuisine with a sophisticated flare, combining French and Asian accents with Northwestern fare. Chef Machura's philosophy is to use local and organically grown ingredients whenever they are available. Start your meal with a serving of Crab Cakes with Kimchee and Lemon Confit Puree or a Duck Confit Roll with Sweet & Spicy Peanut Sauce. Then nestle into a luscious entrée of Grilled Salmon with Orange Sesame Glaze, Caramelized Fennel Bulb, and Yogurt Risotto, or a thick Elk Chop with Wilted Greens and Roasted Shiitake Mushroom Ketchup. Then finish off your feast with a luscious housemade dessert, or a selection of artisan cheeses and fruit.

The award-winning wine list offers a wide selection of fine American wines, along with many international selections, as well as many hard-to-find boutique wineries.

A trip to Big Sky is not complete without a venture to Moonlight Basin and a meal at The Timbers.

Y Award of Excellence

There are fabulous views for outside dining.

Warm Quail Salad
With Mangos, Figs, and Honey Rosemary Vinaigrette

Ingredients

4 4-ounce quail
2 ripe mangos

½ pound mixed greens
12-15 black mission figs, dried

Preparation

PEEL mangos and slice in half, avoiding large oval pit inside. Slice each half into slivers and set aside. Slice the figs in half and set those aside as well.

RUB quails with olive oil, salt, and pepper. Grill until just cooked through inside the breast area. Slice quail in half and place on top of greens with the sliced mangos, figs, and vinaigrette.

For the Vinaigrette

4 cups grapeseed oil
2 tablespoons champagne vinegar (or any white vinegar)
3 tablespoons honey

1 teaspoon soy sauce
1 tablespoon fresh rosemary, finely chopped
   Salt and white pepper to taste

COMBINE all ingredients in blender and purée until smooth and combined.

Serves 4

Beet Salad
Thinly sliced Red Beets with Roasted Golden Beets, Watercress, and Olive Oil

Ingredients

4 medium-sized red beets, washed and peeled
4 medium-sized golden beets, washed
¾ cup olive oil

½ pound watercress, washed and stems removed
1 12-ounce bottle white truffle oil (if available in your area)

PREHEAT oven to 350°F. Slice the red beets as thin as possible and marinate with just enough of the olive oil to coat. Set aside. Rub the golden beets with a bit more of the olive oil, some salt and pepper, and roast approximately 1½ hours until they slide off of a paring knife like a potato. Let cool and slice into wedges. Lay out red beets on plate. Toss roasted golden beets, watercress, salt and pepper, a bit of the olive oil, and truffle oil to moisten and place on top of the red beets.

Serves 6

GRILLED 13-MILE FARM LEG OF LAMB
with Truffle Parsnip Puree, Asparagus, and Mint Aioli

Many people still enjoy mint with their lamb, and this is the Timber's creative way of serving mint and lamb together. At our restaurant, we use 13-Mile Farm lamb from Belgrade. We break down the legs into each of the seven muscles and then grill them.

Ingredients

1 Leg of Lamb
Truffle Parsnip Puree (recipe follows)

Mint Aioli (recipe follows)

BREAK leg of lamb into the seven muscles and grill over hot cools until desired temperature is achieved.

TO SERVE, place grilled lamb on service plates, with serving of Truffle Parsnip Puree to the side, and place a portion of Mint Aioli on top of lamb.

Serves 4

For the Truffle Parsnip Puree

10 parsnips, peeled and cut into 1-inch pieces
2 tablespoons soft butter

⅓ cup heavy cream
1 tablespoon truffle oil
salt and pepper to taste

STEAM parsnip until completely tender. Mash as you would potatoes. Add butter, cream, truffle oil, and salt and pepper to taste.

For the Mint Aioli

2 egg yolks
1 tablespoon lemon juice
1 cup grapeseed oil

½ cup finely diced mint
salt and pepper to taste

PLACE yolks and lemon juice in a bowl. While whisking constantly, slowly add oil until mixture is white and creamy like a mayonnaise. Add mint and adjust seasonings with salt and pepper.

The Continental Divide

East Main Street
Ennis, Montana
406-682-7600

Open for Dinner
May 1 to Mid-October
Hours: 6:00 to 10:00 pm

The Continental Divide

Eric and Marzena Trapp, Owners
Eric Trapp, Chef

The Continental Divide was opened in the summer of 1982 by Jay and Karen Bentley and was acquired by Eric and Marzena Trapp in 1999. It began as a small, seasonal fine-dining restaurant catering mostly to the fly-fishing enthusiasts that visit Montana each year. French and Creole cuisine was the culinary theme, emphasizing an experience that was difficult to find elsewhere in Montana at the time. Seating only 30-40 people depending on weather, casual elegance, and quality helped the business to develop an outstanding reputation. The Continental Divide has been reviewed by *The New York Times*, *Esquire Magazine*, *House & Garden*, *Big Sky Journal*, *Bugle Magazine*, and continues to get consistently rave reviews.

The new owners, recognizing that fine cuisine in Montana is no longer rare, are committed to providing fine food paired with excellent wines in a relaxing dining experience. Local organic produce and free range poultry, local wild mushrooms, only wild fresh fish, exotic game, aged U.S.D.A Prime beef, all are painstakingly sought after and carefully prepared. Although small, the wine list is designed not only to match the cuisine but to offer many boutique selections as well as familiar favorites. The Continental Divide opens the first of May and is open until mid-October every summer for dinner only. From July 4th weekend to Labor Day there is also a "Live" Jazz Sunday brunch weather permitting. Dining at the Continental Divide is summed up by their motto "EAT, MEET, & FISH."

Lapin á la Moutarde
(Rabbit with Mustard)

People often steer away from eating rabbit because of its well deserved reputation for being dry. This method is my favorite for many meats, but especially for rabbit.

Ingredients

1 rabbit per every three or four people, cut into even pieces (6-8 pieces per rabbit depending on the size)
Lots of rendered duck fat (may substitute with an oil, but try not to)

Curing spice rub; for rabbit I use fresh thyme, rosemary, sage, dried red chile, black pepper, and salt

MIX to your taste, but not too much salt, sage, or red pepper, as they overwhelm.

Sauce

⅓ cup Dijon mustard
½ cup white wine
1 tablespoon fresh shallots

1 tablespoon fresh garlic
2 tablespoons crème fraîche
White pepper

Preparation for the Sauce (Keeps a few days)

SWEAT minced shallots and garlic in a heavy saucepan, and before they brown, add mustard. Stir constantly for about half a minute to mellow the mustard and add wine. Reduce by one-third. Add crème fraîche, simmer a few minutes, add a pinch of white pepper, and strain through a fine sieve. Reserve in a squeeze bottle. (If you can't buy crème fraîche make your own. To a quart of heavy fresh cream, add 1/4 cup of buttermilk and let sit in a warm spot [65-80°F] until it sets up and then refrigerate.)

RUB the rabbit pieces generously with spice mix and reserve in a steel or glass pan. Overnight is best, 8-12 hours. Take cured pieces and lightly brush them off with your hands, leave a thin layer on the rabbit. Place rabbit in a large baking dish and completely submerge in rendered duck fat. Then place in a 200-220°F oven for 4-7 hours until the meat wants to fall from the bone; but doesn't quite. Gently place the rabbit on a draining rack (a cake cooling rack works great). At this point you can refrigerate the rabbit and reheat later in the oven at medium heat, or serve right away.

I like to serve this with Israeli Couscous and roasted vegetables, but many combinations work well. Arrange the rabbit on plates with side dishes and "paint" it with the sauce from the squeeze bottle. A trick to this is to hold the bottle high and work quickly, not trying to be perfect but to have fun with it. I think this dish demands a nice red burgundy wine—a good Croze-Hermitage or Cote D'Beaune at least.

BROILED FOIE GRAS
with Tobikko Caviar on Roasted Garlic Toast

I love appetizers! Even though they can be time-consuming to prepare, and often a very high-cost food item, the Continental Divide always offers an interesting array. Guests often join us just for these items and a nice glass of wine. This classicly simple recipe is rarely on the menu, and was created expressly for the birthday of one of our favorite people. Her husband rented the entire restaurant and invited many of the local fishing guides and restaurant regulars. It is easy to make, and has gorgeous contrast. Pair with a crisp, flinty Chardonnay; Neyers Reserve, Les Pierres from Sonoma Cutrer, or your favorite 1st Cru French Chablis.

Ingredients

- 3 ounces (per person) fresh foie gras, a good grade B+ will do nicely.
- 2 slices (per person) bread for toasting, allow for mistakes. (I prefer "English Muffin Toasting Bread" in the Blue and White wrapper.) But any white sliced bread will suffice.

- ½ ounce (per person) fresh Orange Tobikko
  Roasted Garlic Oil, I make my own by simmering peeled garlic cloves in good olive oil, but you don't have to.

Preparation

FIRST cut crusts off of the bread. Then cut four points per slice: Cut from right bottom corner to the middle of the opposite side, repeat from left side, then from point of remaining piece cut in half. This should create four identical long pointy triangles. Brush lightly with garlic oil and toast under broiler until golden brown and crunchy. Don't over-oil them as the Foie Gras is already rich. This can be done a few hours ahead, but leave uncovered so they stay dry.

CAREFULLY pull any veins and connective tissue from the Foie Gras and slice into fairly regular ¼-inch slices. Pull any remaining veins as you go. Reserve Foie Gras on a baking sheet with four sides (to prevent oil spillage). One trick is to make sure the Foie Gras is very cold, but not frozen, to facilitate slicing. Cut any very big pieces down to fit on the toast points. This doesn't have to be exact. Open the Tobikko and get a small plastic or glass spoon to handle it.

NEXT, decorate your serving platter or appetizer plate. I like something minimalistic but decadent to reflect the nature of the dish. Little edible viola flowers or a squash blossom for example. Place the Foie Gras under a hot broiler until reduced in size (roughly one-fourth to one-fifth). There will be loads of rendered fat left. You should save this for other uses. With tongs, very gently lay the pieces on the toast points, combining if needed to cover them at least by two-thirds. This is the trickiest part. Don't break the points or crush the Foie Gras. Next balance a generous spoon of Tobikko on top of every piece and arrange on the platter or dish. The neon of the Tobikko, the smooth richness of the Foie Gras, and the crisp crunch of the garlic toasts, followed by the lingering popping of the Tobikko will delight even your guests who say they "hate liver." Be sure to make more than you think you'll need.

Potosi Hot Springs Resort

1 South Willow Creek Road
6½ miles south of Pony, Montana
406-685-3330 or 1-888-685-1695
www.potosiresort.com
Open year-round, 7 days a week,
24 hours a day

Hot springs and other facilities are for
overnight guests only.
The restaurant is open for dinner to
the public for groups of 8 or more
(advance reservation required)

Potosi Hot Springs

Christine & Nick Kern, Owners
Christine Kern, Chef

The area where Potosi Hot Springs Resort is located has a wild history. There are tipi rings in the area, evidence that Native American tribes must have occupied this region and must have also enjoyed the healing properties and comfort of the hot springs. There is even evidence that these mountains were mined as far back as the 1600s by Spanish explorers. However, the modern history of Potosi dates back to the late 1800s when the area was developing as a gold mining hotbed. Virginia City was the state capital at that time, and Butte was the biggest city in the territory. Pony at one time had a population of about 2,000-4,000 people, whereas today there are only about 75 year-round residents. President Taft signed the Placer Mining Claims that currently make up the property of Potosi Hot Springs Resort.

This 75-acre in holding in the Beaverhead-Deerlodge National Forest was set off primarily to become a resort, with the focus on the hot springs. There was a 14-room lodge built in the 1880s on the same site as the current main lodge. This beautiful old hotel and restaurant

was accessed by cart and buggy only. The owner would drive down the 6 1/2-mile dirt road to pick up guests at the train line that spurred off from Harrison and came into Pony. This remote lodge prospered for a number of years until it was sold in the 1930s or 1940s to a local rancher who moved the structure to his ranch. The building was later sold off for lumber. From the day that the hotel was removed, the area became a public place for camping, picnicking, and enjoying the hot spring pool that had been built in 1892. The area remained this way until the 1960s.

At some point the canyon became the home to a "hippie commune." They apparently moved in and settled in the canyon past the springs. The locals felt they had lost their spot, and in order to get the group to leave, blew up the walls of the pool with dynamite.

Potosi Hot Springs, Pony

104

In the mid-1970s Pete and Virginia Gross purchased the property and built a residence what is now the main lodge. They lived here for about 10 years as they developed another hot spring and rebuilt the walls to the pool (the floor of the pool is still the original floor poured in 1892). They eventually sold the property to the Trapp family, who lived in the residence for four years before deciding to build the four cabins and make a business out of it.

Nick & Christine Kern , Owners.

On April 7, 2000 Nick Kern and Christine Stark became the new owners of this truly amazing property. Since the purchase they have made a number of improvements, including a new hot springs and a sauna. They have also managed to build a strong, steady business, which has gained national media attention as well as a fantastic "word of mouth" reputation. In the fall of 2004, Nick and Christine completed their business and personal partnership with their marriage.

The updated Potosi Hot Springs Resort combines mountain seclusion with luxury accommodations and excellent gourmet, Western cuisine, providing the ultimate Montana escape.

Potosi offers guests a wide variety or activities year-round: guided fly-fishing trips, horsepack trips, nature hikes, historic tours, mountain biking, whitewater rafting, and many

other outdoor adventures are all available through the resort. In the fall, the guided hunting opportunities are abundant. In the winter, Potosi Hot Springs Resort offers a pristine playground for snowshoeing, cross-country skiing, and backcountry skiing/snowboarding expeditions to the high alpine peaks that surround the resort. Any time of year is an ideal time to stay at Potosi Hot Springs Resort.

The Potosi Hotel before 1918.

STEAMED ARTICHOKE WITH PECAN-HERB AIOLI

Enjoy this as a dramatic but very easy first course, or bring it to your next potluck party.

Ingredients

1 large artichoke, leaves trimmed and
  stem cut to base
1 cup plain nonfat soy yogurt
½ cup mayonnaise
  juice of 1 lemon
½ cup pecans, chopped
1 tablespoon lemon thyme, chopped

1 tablespoon parsley, chopped
1 tablespoon basil, chopped
1 tablespoon chives, chopped
  salt and freshly ground pepper to taste
  small amount of olive oil to finish
  lemon wedges for garnish
  additional chopped herbs for garnish

Preparation

PLACE artichoke stem side down in saucepan. Add 1-½ inches of cold water. Bring to a boil; turn down to a simmer and cover. Steam artichoke for about 30 minutes. Remove from pan and let cool upside down.

MIX remaining ingredients, except the garnishes and olive oil, in a bowl and taste. Add salt and pepper as needed. Refrigerate until ready to stuff artichoke.

TO FINISH, remove the inner "choke" from the artichoke by lightly pulling back the outer leaves and pulling out the very center leaves, which are very pale and almost transparent. Discard the inner leaves and, using a spoon, scoop out the bottom fuzzy choke. Spoon the pecan herb mixture into the hollowed center, drizzle and little olive oil over the top. Garnish with the lemon wedges and chopped herbs.

Serves 2 to 4

Wine Suggestions: Schramsberg Blanc de Blanc Brut (sparkling)
Gary Farrell Chardonnay, Russian River 2001

POTOSI'S POACHED TROUT

For the Trout

3 whole rainbow trout
2 cups white wine
6 tablespoons unsalted butter, cut into
   ¼-inch pieces
6 sprigs fresh dill
   Salt and pepper

Two lemons, one thinly sliced, one for garnish
Cooking spray
Aluminum foil: 6 sheets, about 12 inches square

Preparation

PREHEAT oven to 350°F.

PLACE two pieces of foil on top of each other, roll edges together on one side, and open the foil pieces like a book. Spray the inside of the foil with cooking spray and set aside, with rolled edge facing away. Using a very sharp knife, remove the head just behind the gills, and slice the trout into two filets, along the backbone and through the tail. Trim the fins off the body. Rinse well under cold water and pat dry with paper towels. Place each trout filet skin side down on foil. Top with butter pieces, dill sprig, and 3-4 lemon slices. Sprinkle salt and pepper on top. Slightly fold edges of foil upwards, and carefully pour about ½ cup of white wine into the packet. Roll the remaining three edges of foil packet together, and cut a slit into the top to allow for steam release during the cooking process. Repeat this process for remaining filets. These packets can be cooked on a grill over medium heat about 8-10 minutes or on a tray in your oven at about 350°F for 8-10 minutes. Be careful letting steam escape when opening the cooked trout packets!

To serve

REMOVE the cooked lemons and dill, then replace the lemon slices on top of the filets when ready to serve.

RISOTTO, a fresh green salad, roasted potatoes, grilled veggies or corn-on-the-cob are delicious with this dish. The options are endless!

Serves 6

POTOSI'S LIME TART
with Chambord Cream and Berries

For the Crust

    1 *package graham crackers*
    ½ *cup macadamia nuts, shelled and whole*

    2 *tablespoons unsalted butter*
        10-inch tart pan with removable bottom

For the Filling

    2 *teaspoons lime zest (use rasp or zester)*
        Juice of 8 large limes

    6 *large eggs*
    1½ *cups white sugar*
    1 *cup unsalted butter*

For the Garnish

    3 *cups heavy cream*
    ¼ *cup Chambord (raspberry liqueur)*
    3 *tablespoons powdered sugar*

    ½ *pint fresh raspberries*
    24 *pieces lime peel*

Preparation

PREHEAT oven to 325°F.

COMBINE graham crackers and macadamia nuts in food processor, and pulse into small crumbs. Melt 2 tablespoons butter in medium bowl in microwave, then add crumb mixture to melted butter. Stir with fork until crumbs are evenly moistened, and transfer crumb mixture to tart pan. Press crumb mixture into the sides of the pan, and firmly into the bottom. Bake at 325°F for about 10 minutes, or until crust is golden brown. Remove from oven and let cool.

COMBINE lime juice, 1 cup butter, and ½ cup sugar in saucepan. Melt mixture over very low heat, stirring occasionally. In separate bowl, add eggs, remaining sugar, and lime zest, and whisk until well blended. When saucepan mixture has melted, slowly add to egg mixture, whisking continually. Add this combined mixture back into saucepan, turn heat up to medium, and whisk continually until it slightly thickens, about 3-5 minutes. Remove from heat and gently pour mixture into tart pan. Put tart into refrigerator uncovered for about 2 hours. Then cover well with plastic wrap, and refrigerate another 4-6 hours before serving.

Presentation

WHIP the heavy cream, Chambord and powdered sugar in a bowl (or standing mixer) until thick. Place tart slice on small plate, spoon cream over, and arrange raspberries on the plate with lime peel.

Serves 10-12

Big Hole Lodge

CRAIG FELLIN & BIG HOLE
OUTFITTERS & LODGE

P.O. Box 156
Wise River, MT 59762
www.flyfishinglodge.com
bigholeriver@montana.com

Dining available for lodge
guests only

Craig Fellin Outfitters & Big Hole Lodge

Anglers from all over the world come to Craig Fellin's Big Hole Lodge to catch storied rainbows, browns and cutthroats on Montana's fabled trout streams: the Big Hole, and the Beaverhead. They also come to enjoy the beauty of Montana; relaxing in the luxurious lodge, hiking the beautiful pine-covered hills, and enjoying sumptuous meals in the lodge dining room.

The lodge is nestled in a magnificent wilderness setting with a stream outside the door. The main lodge is built from local lodge-pole pine and offers a spectacular view of the Rocky Mountains. Guest cabins are spacious, with rustic, western fixtures and accents. All accommodations are designed to offer an intimate experience for the guests.

Big Hole Lodge will spoil you with three gourmet meals a day prepared by Chef Lanette Evener, who is famous throughout the West for her cuisine. Lanette has been with the Big Hole Lodge since 1993, assuming the position of Chef in 1996. She has also worked at a California ski resort and has increased her culinary knowledge with courses at the Culinary Center of Monterey. When not working to make your meals a true dining experience, Lanette can be found on a trout stream.

During your stay, you will be treated to sumptuous meals such as pine nut crusted halibut with wild rice, topped with a white peach salsa in a port wine butter sauce; and then finish with a ginger crème brulee for dessert. Lunch could be marinated tip roast on a fresh baked roll with Mexican corn, ending with a sweet and tart lemon bar. The lodge has an extensive wine cellar with fine California wines. Craig Fellin's Big Hole Lodge offers its guests a great fishing experience and is also a culinary delight.

Big Hole Lodge, Wise River

Goat Cheese, Prosciutto, Sage, and Puff Pastry Pinwheels

Ingredients

8 ounces goat cheese, room temperature
2 5" x 5" puff pastry sheets, thawed
6 slices prosciutto
4 tablespoons fresh sage, minced

1 egg, beaten – for egg wash
salt and pepper to taste
cooking spray

Preparation

HEAT oven to 400 degrees. On a flat surface, lat out the thawed puff pastry sheets. Using a rolling pin, roll dough to ⅛-inch thickness, keeping the dough square. Spread 4 ounces of goat cheese on each puff pastry sheet, leaving ½ inch at the top edge. Place 3 slices of prosciutto on top of the cheese and sprinkle with half the sage, adding salt and pepper to taste. Brush egg wash on top ½ inch edge of each pastry sheet.

FROM the bottom, roll each puff pastry into cylinder. With the seam side down, slice each cylinder into ¼ to ⅜ inch thick pinwheels. Spray a baking sheet with cooking spray and place pinwheels at least 2 inches apart. Bake in center of 400-degree oven for 18 to 20 minutes, until golden.

Serves 12 to 16

The dining room at Big Hole Lodge.

ROASTED GARLIC AND BRIE SOUP
with Fresh Herbs

Ingredients

2   whole garlic bulbs
5   tablespoons olive oil, divided
    salt and pepper, to taste
1   medium onion, finely diced
3   celery stalks, finely diced
2   carrots, finely diced

¼   cup flour
6   cups chicken stock
2   teaspoons fresh oregano, chopped
1   teaspoon fresh thyme, chopped
8   ounces Brie cheese

Preparation

HEAT the oven to 350 degrees. Cut the top ¼ inch off the garlic bulbs to expose cloves. Place garlic, cut side up, in a small baking dish. Add 2 tablespoons of olive oil and sprinkle with salt and pepper. Cover tightly with aluminum foil. Bake garlic bulbs until cloves are tender to the touch, about 50 minutes. Let cool. Squeeze cloves into a small bowl and set aside.

IN A large saucepan, heat remaining 3 tablespoons olive oil. Add onion and sauté until translucent, about 10 minutes. Add celery and carrot, sautéing for another 10 minutes. Stir in the flour and cook for 3 minutes more. Gradually stir in the chicken stock and bring to a boil. Reduce heat to a simmer and let cook until slightly thickened, about 15 minutes, stirring occasionally.

IN A blender, combine the roasted garlic with one cup of soup and purée. Add purée back to soup. Stir in fresh oregano and thyme and continue to simmer soup. Remove rind from the Brie and chop into pieces. Gradually add Brie to soup, stirring until it has melted. Season with salt and pepper to taste.

Serves 6

GRILLED APPLE AND ROQUEFORT SALAD

with Candied Walnuts and Port Vinaigrette

Ingredients

1 green apple, chilled
   olive oil
2 cups peanut oil
1 cup walnut halves
1 teaspoon Kosher salt
1 cup confectioner's sugar
2 cups port wine

1 shallot, minced
3 tablespoons red wine vinegar
6 tablespoons extra virgin olive oil
10 ounces mixed spring greens
6 ounces Roquefort cheese, crumbled
   salt and pepper to taste

Preparation

HEAT grill to medium heat. Cut the apple into quarters, remove the stem and seeds, and cut into ⅛ inch thick slices. Spray or brush both sides with olive oil and set aside.

IN A deep fryer or a deep pot, heat the peanut oil to 350 degrees. Meanwhile, in a large saucepan bring 2 quarts of water to a boil. Add the walnut halves and boil for 2 minutes. Drain in a strainer, shaking off any excess water. Sprinkle with salt and then coat them with the confectioner's sugar, a little at a time, allowing the sugar to melt onto the walnuts. Toss the nuts by shaking the strainer, adding a little more sugar at a time, until the sugar is used and the walnuts are coated and glazed over. Carefully add the walnuts to the heated oil, maintaining the oil at 350 degrees. Cook the walnuts until golden brown, about 3 minutes, stirring occasionally. Remove the walnuts with a slotted spoon onto a baking sheet and let cool.

IN A medium saucepan, bring port wine and the shallot to a boil, lower heat and simmer until reduced by half, about 5 to 10 minutes. Remove from heat and let cool. Whisk in vinegar and extra virgin olive oil until emulsified. Add salt and pepper to taste.

USING tongs, lay apple slices, carefully, on preheated grill and grill 1 minute per side, just until golden grill marks are apparent.

COMBINE the mixed greens and port wine vinaigrette in a salad bowl. Season lightly with salt and pepper and toss. To serve, divide the salad among 4 plates and sprinkle with the walnut halves, crumbled Roquefort and fan the apples slices on top.

Serves 4

GRILLED CEDAR PLANKED SALMON

with Whole Grain Mustard Sauce, Mushroom Sauté, and Basmati Pilaf

This very old Pacific Northwest method of cooking fish has been on the menu at Craig Fellin Outfitters and Big Hole Lodge for many years and is a client favorite. Please note, you will need to soak the cedar plank in water for at least 4 hours or up to 1 day before grilling.

Ingredients

2½ pounds wild salmon, preferably cut as a long fillet, about 18 inches long
1 20-inch untreated cedar plank, specially made for food preparation
½ cup dry white wine
1 tablespoon lemon zest
  salt and pepper

Basmati Rice Pilaf (recipe follows)
Mushroom Sauté (recipe follows)
Whole Grain Mustard Sauce (recipe follows)
6 lemon wedges for garnish
6 basil sprigs for garnish

Preparation

IMMERSE the cedar plank in water, soaking it from 4 to 24 hours. Place salmon skin side down on a baking sheet. Pour white wine over salmon and sprinkle with lemon zest, salt, and pepper. Marinate in the refrigerator for 30 minutes.

HEAT the grill to 350 degrees. Remove salmon from baking sheet and place it on the soaked cedar plank, skin side down. When the grill is ready, place the planked salmon in center of cooking grate and cook 25 to 30 minutes, or until the salmon is opaque in the center and the flesh flakes easily with a fork. Flip salmon over and slowly peel back the skin, if you wish. Slice salmon into 4 to 6 pieces.

TO SERVE, place ½ cup Basmati Rice Pilaf in the center of each plate. Place 1 salmon fillet on top of the pilaf. Place the Mushroom Sauté on one half side of the salmon, falling off and around the salmon. Pour Whole Grain Mustard Sauce on the other half of the salmon and around it. Place 1 basil sprig on top of the salmon and 1 lemon wedge on the side.

For the Basmati Rice Pilaf

1 tablespoon olive oil
2 tablespoons onion, diced
2 tablespoons celery, diced
1 cup basmati rice

1 bay leaf
1½ cups chicken stock
  pinch of salt

IN A medium saucepan over medium heat, add olive oil, onion, and celery. Cook 1 minute. Add the rice and cook for a few minutes or until some of the rice grains begin to brown. Add the bay leaf, chicken stock, and salt. Bring to a boil and boil for 2 minutes. Reduce heat to low, cover, and cook pilaf until rice is tender and stock is absorbed, about 25 to 30 minutes. Fluff with a fork and keep warm.

For the Mushroom Sauté

2 tablespoons fresh basil leaves, minced
¼ cup fresh parsley leaves, minced
3 cloves garlic, minced and divided
5 tablespoons extra virgin olive oil, divided

½ teaspoon Kosher salt
2 pounds assorted mushrooms (such as chanterelles, shiitakes, morels, crimini, and portobello)
1 tablespoon fresh lemon juice

IN A small bowl, combine the basil and parsley with 1 of the minced garlic cloves; set aside. In a large bowl, whisk together the other 2 minced garlic cloves, 4 tablespoons of the olive oil and the salt. Depending on the types of mushrooms that you use, quarter the large mushrooms and halve the medium ones. Add the mushrooms to the garlic & olive oil mix and toss to coat.

HEAT the remaining tablespoon of olive oil in a sauté pan over high heat. Add the mushroom mixture and sauté until mushrooms are tender and browned, about 10 minutes. Remove the skillet from heat and mix in the basil/parsley mixture along with the lemon juice. Season to taste with salt and pepper and keep warm.

For the Whole Grain Mustard Sauce

2 teaspoons butter
¼ cup onion, minced
½ cup dry white wine

2 tablespoons whole grain mustard (preferably Maille)
1 cup heavy cream

IN A medium saucepan over medium heat, melt the butter. Add onion and cook 1 minute. Add white wine, stir and reduce by half. Stir in whole grain mustard and heavy cream and reduce by one quarter, stirring occasionally. Keep warm.

Serves 4 to 6

Wine Suggestion: 2003 St. Supery Sauvignon Blanc Napa Valley

Cattle roundup, roping calves, August 1904, Big Dry.

Jackson Hot Springs Lodge

Jackson Hot Springs Lodge

The Peterson Family, Owners
James Eaker & Kelli Bush, Chefs

The tiny cow town at the end of the Big Hole Valley of south-west Montana was named for the town's first postmaster, Antone Jackson. On July 7, 1806, shortly after Lewis and Clark separated during their return from the Pacific Ocean, Clark discovered the hot springs in the Big Hole Valley (which he called "Hot Springs Valley"). Clark and his party, along with their Shoshone Indian guide Sacajawea, settled around the hot springs for their noonday lunch. At this time, Clark cooked a piece of meat "the width of two fingers" in the steaming water, noting that in five minutes the meat was cooked enough to eat and that the water "blubbers with heat for twenty paces below where it rises."

In 1884 Benoit O. Fournier made public claim to the springs where he built his home and a small plunge. Sometime in 1898 the local paper reported that "a bath in the hot water is one of the luxuries which people usually take advantage of when in town."

It was in 1911 that M. D. Jardine purchased the springs and built the first hotel on Main Street, along with a public plunge to which he piped the hot springs water 1,300 feet from its source. In 1950, the resort was purchased by John Dooling, a successful rancher from Jackson Hole, Wyoming. Dooling's dream was to construct a new log inn and hot springs pool, which he completed later that year. Originally named the Diamond Bar Inn, the new lodge cost Dooling approximately $400,000 and quickly became the center of activity of outdoor enthusiasts in the Big Hole Valley. Since the 1960s the lodge has gone through several owners and has been owned by the Peterson family since 1990.

Gleaming woodwork, polished floors, clean, bright hot pool open to the stars, spruced-up grounds, and congenial staff have turned the lodge into a community gathering spot.

CREAMY WILD MUSHROOM SOUP

Our Executive Chef, James Eacker, created this soup. It can be served as described below, with the julienned mushroom pieces, or it can be puréed for a totally different texture and look.

Ingredients

1 cup sweet cream butter, cubed
½ cup shallots, minced
¼ cup garlic cloves, minced
2 cups portabella mushroom caps, julienned
2 cups shiitake mushrooms caps, julienned
1 cup crimini mushroom caps, julienned

1¼ cups all-purpose flour, sifted
1½ cups half and half
1½ cups whole milk, to proper consistency
½ cup dry grated Parmesan cheese
1 teaspoon dried thyme
1 tablespoon dried basil
salt and white pepper to taste

Preparation

PUT butter in large pot over medium heat. Add shallots and garlic; sauté for 2 to 3 minutes. Add all mushroom products and sauté for 4 minutes; then mix well in pot and sauté for another 3 minutes. Add flour and make a roux. Cook on medium heat for 3 minutes or until a nutty smell begins to fill the pot. Slowly incorporate the half and half while mixing, until mixture appears smooth and shiny. Slowly add milk until thinned to proper consistency. Let simmer for 3 minutes, while stirring, and then add Parmesan and dried herbs. Taste and add salt and white pepper as needed.

Serves 4 (6-ounce servings)

BUFFALO NEW YORK STRIP
with Caramelized Garlic Butter Sauce

The first night we prepared this recipe, we sold out!

Ingredients

    4 10 to 12-ounce buffalo New York strip steaks (can substitute any wild game or beef)
    3 tablespoons butter

Steak Seasoning

    2 tablespoons kosher salt or 1
       tablespoon + 1 teaspoon table salt
    1 tablespoon pepper (coarse ground
       black pepper if possible)

    2 teaspoons garlic, granulated or powder
    ¼ teaspoon cayenne pepper
    1 teaspoon granulated onion or onion
       powder

Caramelized Garlic Butter Sauce

    ½ cup thinly sliced garlic (slice thin by
       hand or use smallest blade on food
       processor)
  2-4 tablespoons oil (vegetable or olive oil)
    ¼ teaspoon coarse black pepper or
       cracked black pepper
    ½ teaspoon salt

    ½ cup white wine
    1 tablespoon Worcestershire sauce
    ¼ cup beef stock or beef broth
    1 teaspoon granulated onion or
       powdered onion
    ½ cup butter (cut into pieces)

Cooking Instructions for the Steak

MIX dry steak seasonings together. Sprinkle over both sides of steaks. Let rest. Melt butter in heavy pan over medium heat. When butter begins to brown add seasoned steaks. Cook/brown on both sides 2 minutes. Remove from pan. Put in new pan, slightly buttered. Bake in oven until desired temperature of 350° to 400°F is reached, anywhere from 5 to 15 minutes. While steaks are in oven, make sauce.

For the Caramelized Garlic Butter Sauce

PUT oil in heavy-bottomed pan, over medium heat. When oil is warm add sliced garlic. Sauté, stirring occasionally until golden brown. Add salt, pepper, and wine. Cook for two minutes at medium-high heat. Add beef stock or beef broth, Worcestershire, and granulated onion. Bring to boil then simmer for two minutes. Stir in a couple tablespoons of butter at a time. Stir until completely incorporated before adding additional butter. Repeat. Serve warm sauce over steaks.

Serves 4

SALMON AND SPINACH IN PUFF PASTRY
with Dijon Cream Sauce

So popular over the holidays that we had special requests for dinner parties.

For the Salmon

8   squares of puff pastry, 5 x 6 inches
2   cups fresh spinach leaves
8   tablespoons cream cheese
    Salt and pepper

½   teaspoon crushed red chile pepper
    flakes
¼   teaspoon garlic
4   6-8 ounce pieces of salmon filet

Salmon Cooking Instructions

PREHEAT oven to 350°.

PLACE 4 or 5 leaves of spinach in middle of puff pastry square, place 2 tablespoons of cream cheese in center and sprinkle with salt and pepper. Then sprinkle with red chile pepper flakes and garlic. Place salmon filet on top of the cream cheese and spinach.

SPRINKLE top of salmon filet with salt and pepper. Fold pastry up around sides of salmon. Place additional pastry square over entire stack, slightly stretch to tuck under. Brush with water along seam to seal. Bake in 350° oven for 20 minutes.

Dijon Cream Sauce

½   cup white wine
1   teaspoon of lemon juice
¼   teaspoon fresh garlic, minced
1¼ cups extra heavy whipping cream

2   tablespoons Dijon mustard
¼   teaspoon salt
    Pinch of black pepper

Dijon Cream Sauce Cooking Instructions

IN SAUCEPAN over medium heat put in wine, lemon juice, and minced garlic. Bring to boil. Simmer to reduce by approximately half. Add cream, salt, pepper, and Dijon. Stir well. Simmer for 3 to 4 minutes until slightly thick. Serve sauce warm over Salmon Spinach Pastry.

Serves 4

COWBOY BEEF FILET MIGNON

This entrée was introduced because we wanted a new finish to our filet that would be an enhancement but not overpowering to the meat. We are in beef country, and the distinction of our meats is defined at our dining tables. This dish is offered on our regular menu and continues to be a wonderful seller. Although it is not the nature of this kitchen, to serve any meat "well done," this presentation works wonderfully for the most rare of steaks to the most thoroughly cooked.

Ingredients (per filet)

filet mignon	1 teaspoon garlic, chopped
2 tablespoons butter	1 dash Worcestershire sauce
2 mushrooms, sliced	2 ounces sweet vermouth
1 tablespoon shallots, chopped	2 ounces beef broth
1 tablespoon scallions, chopped	Salt and pepper, a good pinch of each

Preparation

ASK each guest how they would like their filet cooked and grill individual filets. Each filet is made to order and will be finished in the mushroom sauce.

Sauce

SAUTÉ mushrooms, shallots, scallions, and garlic in the butter. Add Worcestershire sauce, sweet vermouth, and beef broth and reduce. Place grilled filet into the sauce reduction, and turn at least once to finish. The sauce should be reduced by half when finished.

Presentation

PLACE filet on serving plate and pour sauce over the filet. The presentation of the natural pour of the sauce over the filet will delight anyone.

Serves 1

SPICY VELVET SHRIMP

Kelli Bush, our Sous Chef, created this luscious recipe.

Ingredients

- ½ pound shrimp, de-shelled and de-veined
- 2 tablespoons olive oil
- 2 tablespoons garlic, minced
- 1 teaspoon fresh rosemary, finely chopped
- 1 tablespoon red pepper flakes
- 1 teaspoon fresh thyme, finely chopped
- ¼ cup Budweiser beer
- 1 teaspoon cayenne pepper
- ½ teaspoon chili powder
- 1 tablespoon whole butter (cold)
  salt and white pepper to taste
- ½ cup cooked rice
  thyme sprigs for garnish (optional)

Preparation

COOK rice as you are cleaning and de-veining the shrimp.

LIGHTLY sauté garlic and olive oil; add shrimp, rosemary, red pepper and thyme. Sauté shrimp until lightly browned and add Budweiser to de-glaze. Add cayenne pepper and chili powder, sauté. Remove from heat, add butter and swirl continuously until butter has melted. Add salt and white pepper to taste.

PLACE a large spoonful of rice in the center of a shallow rimmed bowl. Gently spoon in shrimp and sauce: garnish with a sprig of thyme.

Serves 2

A CHOCOLATE PLUNGE
White Chocolate Mousse with Chocolate Ganache Swirl

First make the ganache, so that it can cool to room temperature while you are making the mousse. Serve the dessert in white wine glasses for an elegant presentation.

Ingredients for the Ganache

1 cup dark chocolate, chopped   ¾ cup fresh heavy cream

Preparation

HEAT heavy cream to a light boil in a heavy-bottomed saucepan, stirring to prevent scorching. Remove from heat, add the chopped dark chocolate, stir and let sit for a few seconds, and then stir again until melted and smooth. Let cool at room temperature, stirring occasionally.

Ingredients for the Mousse

2 cups white chocolate, chopped   1 cup egg whites
½ cup butter   4 tablespoons sugar
¾ cup egg yolks – approximately 7 to 8   1 cup heavy cream

Preparation

HEAT a pan of water to simmer. Place a dry stainless steel bowl on top to create a hot water bath.

MELT the white chocolate, stirring constantly to keep the edges from scorching. Remove bowl from heat, and add butter, stirring until melted and combined.

IN A mixer, whip egg whites with 2 tablespoons of the sugar until it forms a soft peak.

ADD egg yolks to melted chocolate; mix well, and then fold in ¼ of the egg white mixture.

WHIP heavy cream and remainder of sugar to a soft peak. Fold in another ¼ of the egg white mixture into the melted chocolate. Then fold in ½ of the whipped heavy cream, followed by another ¼ of the egg white mixture. Finally, fold in the second half of the cream, followed by the last of the egg white mixture, until all is folded evenly.

DRIZZLE the chocolate ganache into 8 wine glasses. Set the rest of the ganache aside. Then turn the glasses upside down onto parchment paper so that the ganache will make a pattern on the inside of the wine glass. After 5 minutes, turn glass over and fill with the white chocolate mousse, cover and chill for 5 to 6 hours.

RIGHT before serving, gently heat remaining ganache to warm (not hot). Whip in mixer until thick. Place on top of each white chocolate mousse.

Serves 8

Big Hole Crossing

105 Park Street, just off Hwy 43
Wisdom, MT 59761
(406) 689-3800

Nov–April 8am to 8pm daily
May–Oct 7am to 9 pm daily

Big Hole Crossing

Located in the beautiful Big Hole Valley, 60 miles from the nearest sidewalk, the Big Hole Crossing Restaurant is a great place to eat at any time of the year. Captain Clark visited the Big Hole Valley in 1806, followed by trappers and mountain men who gave the valley its name. The word "hole" is the trapper's name for a mountain valley. The trappers were followed by ranchers, who found their cattle becoming exceptionally fat on the rich hay of the valley. The Big Hole Crossing Restaurant comes from the name of the valley, which is 60 miles long and 30 miles wide. The little town of Wisdom was originally known as "The Crossings", since it was the place that the cowboys moved cows across the Big Hole River, originally known as the Wisdom River.

The restaurant is situated within the Wisdom River Gallery Building. The building was built in 1960 as a mercantile and implement dealer, to service the needs of the local ranchers. Cattle and hay remain the primary economics of the valley. In the 70s and early 80s, the building was leased to the US Forest Service. When the Forest Service moved out, the building was bought by Daryll and Kay Jacobson, who have completely renovated the building into a warm environment featuring lots of old barn wood, with comfortable Windsor chairs and a cozy fireplace in the dining room. The Jacobsons run the Wisdom River Gallery in the same building, and guests roam freely between the gallery and the restaurant.

Diane and Dennis Havig moved to Wisdom in 1988. In early 1989, Diane began working in the gallery. The original restaurant in the building was known as Pioneer Mountain Company, owned by Jade Peterson. Between 1989 and 1994, Diane watched the restaurant change hands several times. In 1994, Diane and Dennis decided to take a chance on owning the restaurant themselves, even though they had limited restaurant experience. Diane knew what she liked when she ate out, and wanted to give people the opportunity to eat food that was nutritious as well as delicious. Emphasizing "made from scratch" food, Diane has amassed a collection of great recipes. Some came from the original owner's recipes, and many have been added over the years by the restaurant's employees, as well as by Diane. Dining at the Big Hole Crossing Restaurant is a warm and homey experience, making you feel a part of the friendly western town.

Homemade Chicken Noodle Soup

Our soup is made from whole chicken and Kay Jacobson's homemade noodle recipe. It is easy to make, just don't overwork the dough. If you don't have chicken base, bouillon cubes will work, but will add more salt.

Ingredients

½ whole chicken, or chicken pieces, with bone in
3 quarts water
½ cup onion, diced
2 cups celery, slice

1½ cups carrots, sliced
1 tablespoon parsley, chopped
¼ cup chicken base
1 batch Homemade Noodles (recipe follows)

Preparation

BOIL chicken in 3 quarts of water until chicken is cooked through, approximately 1 hour. Remove chicken pieces from the broth. When chicken is cool enough to handle, remove the skin and bones and discard. Tear the meat into bite-sized pieces, and add back to broth. Add onion, celery, carrot, parsley, and chicken base. Cook for 10 minutes on medium-high heat. Drop Homemade Noodles into soup, making sure they do not clump as they are added. Cook soup for another 15 minutes or until noodles are tender.

For the Homemade Noodles

1 egg
¼ cup milk, plus 1 tablespoon
pinch of salt

1 cup flour
1 tablespoon butter, melted

IN A mixer, slightly mix the egg, milk, salt, and flour. Then add melted butter and continue to mix just until dough forms. Do not keep mixing, or dough will become tough. Let dough rest 10 minutes or so and it will roll out more easily.

ON A floured surface, roll out dough until it is about ¼ centimeter (about ⅛ inch) thick. Using a pizza cutter, cut into ¼-inch wide strips. Cut each strip into 4-inch lengths.

Serves 8

SALMON IN PHYLLO

The most looked-forward-to event at our restaurant is the Festive Affair, typically the second weekend in December. Locals reserve their spots early. Tables are scattered throughout the restaurant and gallery. Decorating becomes an obsession—the husbands just hang on while Diane and Kay go at it.

Food is served buffet style, in courses, beginning with appetizers, then salad and entrées, with dessert the grand finale. Our favorite fish entrée is Salmon in Phyllo.

Ingredients

½ cup butter, melted
8 sheets phyllo dough, thawed
4 salmon fillets (6 oz), skinned
8 tablespoons croutons, crumbed
(recipe follows)

Old Bay Seasoning
salt and pepper
paprika
Dill Sauce (recipe follows)

Preparation

HEAT oven to 350 degrees.

PLACE one sheet of phyllo dough on work surface, with the short side facing you. Keep remaining phyllo dough covered with slightly damp kitchen towel to prevent drying. Brush sheet with butter, sprinkle dough with 1 tablespoon crouton crumbs. Place second sheet of phyllo over the first sheet and brush with butter, then sprinkle with another tablespoon of the crouton crumbs.

PUT salmon fillet on prepared dough, with the short side of the fillet about 1 inch in from edge that is facing you, and 2 to 3 inches from both sides. Sprinkle with 2 or 3 shakes of Old Bay Seasoning, paprika, and lightly with salt and pepper.

PULL close end of phyllo over salmon. Fold sides over this. Then flip salmon away from you on table until encased in phyllo. Place salmon on a 9"x 13" cookie sheet, seam side down, and repeat procedure with remaining fish.

COOK at 350° for 30 minutes until browned.

TO SERVE, place hot phyllo package on serving plate and drizzle with Dill Sauce. Accompany with Seasoned Rice.

For the Croutons

    8 *pieces bread, cut into ½" cubes*   3 *shakes of garlic salt*
    ¼ *cup butter, melted*   6 *shakes of parsley flakes*

HEAT oven to 350 degrees.

MIX bread cubes with butter and spread evenly on 9"x 13" pan. Shake garlic salt and parsley over crumbs. Cook in 350-degree oven for 15 minutes; stir and cook 15 minutes more until golden brown. The croutons should be dry, with no moisture. Use 8 tablespoons in the salmon recipe, and save the rest for a salad topping.

For the Dill Sauce

    1 *cup ranch dressing*   1 *teaspoon dried dill weed*
       juice of 1 fresh lemon

MIX all ingredients well and drizzle over fish.

Serves 4

PRIME RIB

Every Saturday night is Prime Rib Night. We use only certified Angus Beef, which we sear first and cook slowly at 225 degrees. This keeps the juices in and reduces shrinkage.

Ingredients

4-5 *pounds boneless rib eye of beef, the best grade you can get*
1 *beer, any kind*
⅓ *cup soy sauce*
5 *shakes granulated garlic*

5 *shakes garlic salt*
2 *shakes regular salt*
4 *shakes pepper (freshly ground if possible)*
2 *tablespoons parsley flakes*

Preparation

SEAR rib eye in cast iron skillet on all sides. Place the roast in a deep baking dish or other heavy 9"x13" pan.

POUR beer over meat. Add rest of ingredients in order. Cook, uncovered in 225-degree oven for approximately 2 to 2½ hours. Check with oven thermometer. Remove from oven when center registers 125 degrees Fahrenheit on the thermometer.

REMOVE meat from pan and let sit at least 10 minutes. Meat will continue to cook. It will be rare to medium-rare in center and outer cuts will be medium to medium-well.

CUT into desired serving sizes.

Serves 6 to 8 (10-ounce portions)

BUTTERMILK PIE

This is a very sweet custard pie and is especially good straight from the oven. It is very popular among our guests, who voice disappointment when we run out.

Ingredients

3 *large eggs*
2 *cups sugar*
¼ *cup flour*
3 *tablespoons butter, melted*

1 *cup buttermilk*
1 *teaspoon vanilla extract*
1 *uncooked piecrust (½ of Pie Crust Recipe under Rhubarb Cream Pie)*

Preparation

HEAT oven to 350 degrees.

IN A mixing bowl, beat eggs until lightly colored. Gradually add sugar, and beat until the mixture becomes thick. With mixer set at lowest speed, blend in flour and melted butter. Do not over blend. Slowly add buttermilk and vanilla. Pour filling into uncooked piecrust. Flute edge of piecrust. Cover edges of pie with tin foil to keep from over-cooking.

BAKE pie in 350-degree oven until golden brown and firm for about 1 hour 20 minutes to 1 hour 30 minutes. Remove the foil around the edge of the piecrust during the last 15 to 20 minutes.

Serves 8 to 10

The Big Hole River.

RHUBARB CREAM PIE

The secret to our pies is a thin piecrust. The focus is on the filling.

When available, we make the pie from the rhubarb that is harvested in Wisdom. Rhubarb is one of the few fruits that will actually grow at 6,000 feet. The recipe, from Lois Grube, gives the delicious tart flavor of rhubarb yet cuts the bite.

Ingredients

3   eggs, slightly beaten
1½ cups sugar
¼   cup flour
½   teaspoon nutmeg
4-5 cups fresh rhubarb, chopped – if using
     frozen: thawed and drained

1   uncooked Pie Crust (recipe follows)
     egg wash, made with 1 beaten egg
     and a little water

Preparation

HEAT oven to 375 degrees.

IN A large bowl, place the slightly beaten eggs. Add the sugar, flour and nutmeg, stirring to combine. Then add the rhubarb, stirring again to coat the chunks. Place the rolled out pie dough into a pie pan, leaving an overlapping edge. Pour the filling into the pan and top with the rest of the pie dough, cut in strips, to form a lattice crust. Flute edge of crust, cover with egg wash, and then cover the edge of the crust with foil, to keep it from over cooking.

BAKE pie for 50 to 60 minutes in a 375-degree oven. Remove foil and continue to bake an additional 15 to 20 minutes until crust is golden brown and filling is bubbly.

Serves 8 to 10

For the Pie Crust

1   cup flour
¼   teaspoon salt

¼   cup shortening
¼ + cup orange juice

IN A mixing bowl, combine the flour and salt. Cut in the shortening to make a fine, crumbly mixture. Add the orange juice, 1 tablespoon at a time. Work mixture until it sticks together, but do not knead too much to avoid making the dough tough.

Yield 1 2-crust pie crust

Triple
Creek
Ranch

5551 West Fork Road
Darby, Montana
Please call ahead
406-821-4600 Fax: 406-821-4666
tcr@bitterroot.net
www.triplecreekranch.com

Open year-round
Dining Room open to public
(depending on availability)
Reservations 6:00 to 8:30 pm

Triple Creek Ranch

Barbara and Craig Barrett, Owners
Judy and Wayne Kilpatrick, General Managers
Melissa Williams, Executive Chef

Main lodge.

Triple Creek Ranch, an internationally renowned Relais & Chateaux property, is an exceptional destination resort for discerning travelers who desire a small world-class facility near Montana's spectacular outdoor activities. Located in the Bitterroot Mountain Range of the Montana Rockies, Triple Creek Ranch is situated on 450 acres of wooded hillside bordered by national forest in three directions.

The original owner purchased the land that is now Triple Creek Ranch in 1982 and built what he believed to be the ideal mountain retreat. Many-time guests, Barbara and Craig Barrett of Arizona purchased Triple Creek Ranch in September 1993. General managers Judy and Wayne Kilpatrick have been full-time residents on the ranch since its beginning.

Triple Creek Ranch boasts 19 beautifully appointed cabins nestled under towering Ponderosa pines. All cabins have wood-burning fireplaces, direct dial phones with separate dataports, voice mail, satellite television, VCR, and a fully stocked bar. Some cabins feature a separate living room and bedroom, steam shower, and hot tub on the deck. Freshly baked cookies are delivered daily to cabins.

Guests enjoy a variety of exhilarating year-round outdoor adventures. In winter they ride horseback through fresh powder, snowshoe along a ridgeline, or snowmobile the high country. Excellent skiing, both cross-country and downhill, is just 30 minutes away. For relaxation, options include experiencing a private in-cabin massage, enjoying the soothing hot tub in the pine-scented forest, or curling up with a good book beside a crackling fire. An on-ranch fitness center is available for those who wish to stay in shape. Popular summer activities include hiking, tennis, fly fishing, whitewater rafting, swimming, horseback rides, cattle drives, and ATV rides. Golfers practice on

Main lodge dining room.

the ranch putting green and then play golf in nearby Hamilton. Some guests choose to take in the majestic mountain views on a Hummer ride. History buffs learn Native American culture or trace the trail of Lewis and Clark on a guided tour. With binoculars in hand, wildlife enthusiasts spy on elk, white-tailed and mule deer, moose, and wild turkeys that live on the ranch. A few even experience the thrill of sighting mountain lion cubs, bald eagles, and on a rare day, an elusive golden eagle.

At the center of Triple Creek Ranch sits an impressive log-and-cedar lodge straddling a picturesque creek. Edged by enormous picture windows and tiers of balcony decks, the soaring structure shelters a rooftop lounge, a library, and an intimate dining room, and serves as the focal point for social activity.

In the evening, guests sample hors d'oeuvres and fine wine while visiting in the lounge. World-class cuisine is savored in the candlelit

Fine dining in an elegant setting.

dining room with entrées such as Herb Crusted Rack of Lamb coated with rosemary, Dijon mustard and Panko, served with black truffle potato purée and merlot-thyme jus. A stroll under the dazzling starlit big sky of Montana ends the perfect day at Triple Creek Ranch.

Melissa Williams, Executive Chef.

MAINE DIVER SCALLOPS THREE WAYS

Shaved Black Truffles and Truffle Oil, Orange Tobiko Crème Fraiche and Micro Greens,
Melted Leeks with Prosciutto

Ingredients

6 large diver scallops equal in size
1 tablespoon olive oil
  kosher salt to taste
  white pepper to taste (optional)
  Shaved Black Truffles and Truffle Oil
  (recipe follows)

Orange Tobiko Crème Fraiche and
Micro Greens (recipe follows)
Melted Leeks with Prosciutto (recipe
follows)

Preparation

IN A heavy skillet, heat olive oil almost until smoking. Season each scallop on both sides with kosher salt. If preferred, lightly season with white pepper. Pan sear scallops until heavily caramelized on each side. Remove from skillet and keep warm

For the Shaved Black Truffles and Truffle Oil

3 thin slices black truffle

½ teaspoon white truffle oil (choose one
  with great aromatics)

SHAVE the truffle slices and place in the truffle oil, making sure to coat the shavings completely. Set aside.

For the Orange Tobiko Crème Fraiche and Micro Greens

1 teaspoon orange Tobiko (or caviar if
  available)
¼ cup sour cream
¼ cup heavy cream

fresh squeezed lime juice, to taste
kosher salt to taste
⅛ cup micro watercress (can also use
  fresh chervil or parsley)

WHIP together the sour cream and heavy cream. Season with lime juice and kosher salt to taste. This will make more Crème Fraiche than you need. In a small bowl, place 2 teaspoons of the Crème Fraiche and stir in the orange Tobiko. Set aside, along with the watercress until serving time.

For the Melted Leeks with Prosciutto

½ leek, blanched and julienned
1 teaspoon butter

1 ounce prosciutto, sliced thin and
  julienned

IN A small skillet, render the prosciutto until crispy. Remove a fourth of the prosciutto from the skillet and set aside. Add the blanched leeks and a teaspoon of butter to the pan with the remaining prosciutto and sauté until done. Season with kosher salt. Remove from heat and keep warm until ready to serve.

To Serve as an Appetizer

PLACE the first scallop on the plate and place ½ of the truffle shavings with a dab of truffle oil. For the second scallop, place about a teaspoon of Crème Fraiche mixed with the Tobiko on the plate and place the scallop on top of that. Top the scallop with the micro watercress or baby fresh herbs. Finally, place ½ of the leeks and prosciutto mix on the plate (about a tablespoon). Place the third scallop on top and place ½ of the crispy Prosciutto on top of the scallop.

To Serve as an Entrée

ALTERNATE each type of scallop to form a circle on a large white round plate. It is very colorful and presents well.

Serves 2 as an Appetizer or 1 as an Entrée

"FOWL PLAY"

Pan Seared Pheasant Breast, Duck Confit and Purple Potato Hash,
with Quail Eggs Over Easy

This recipe is made in 3 different stages for each type of fowl. However, the stock that you make with the pheasant is also used for the Duck Confit and for the final presentation. Read the recipe thoroughly before starting. You will need to make the pheasant stock in advance, and you can also par cook the potatoes.

For the Pan Seared Pheasant (and quick pheasant stock)

Ingredients

1 whole pheasant	1 tablespoon canola oil
1 small carrot, chopped	1 tablespoon duck fat
1 stalk celery, chopped	8 fresh thyme sprigs
½ small onion, chopped	kosher salt to taste
2 cups chicken stock	fresh ground pepper to taste

NOTE: If you have smoked pheasant available, it can be used as a substitute. It would most likely already be cooked so you would only need to heat it. In order to keep it moist, it can be reheated in duck fat.

Preparation

BREAK down the pheasant, reserving the breasts. Use the rest of it to make a quick stock (or only the bones if you would like to use the leg and thigh meat for another application). In a stockpot, roast the bones until nicely caramelized with a small amount of oil, if necessary; and then add the carrots, celery, and onion. Sauté the mixture until the pan is deglazed. Add the chicken stock and reduce by half, or more. Strain and continue to reduce until desired thickness is achieved. Season with kosher salt. Set aside.

SEASON the pheasant breasts with salt and pepper on both sides. In a heavy skillet, heat canola oil on high heat until almost smoking. Sear the pheasant breasts skin side down, until caramelized. Turn over and continue cooking on high heat. When both sides are caramelized, reduce the heat slightly and add duck fat and thyme sprigs to the pan. Continue cooking on the stovetop or in a 450-degree oven, basting often. Remove the pheasant breasts when they are medium to medium well. Cover and keep warm.

For the Duck Confit and Potato Hash

Ingredients

- 8 purple Peruvian fingerling potatoes, small diced and par cooked
- 1 confit of duck leg meat, rough chopped
- 1 teaspoon shallot, minced
- 1 teaspoon garlic, minced
- 1 teaspoon fresh thyme, minced
- 2 ounces pheasant stock
- olive oil
- kosher salt to taste
- fresh ground pepper to taste

NOTE: The potatoes can be par cooked in advance. Follow any recipe for the duck confit. It is generally a 2 to 3 day process, so it will need to be done in advance. Or, you can order duck confit from culinary sources on the Internet.

Preparation

HEAT a small amount of olive oil in a heavy skillet until almost smoking. Add the par-cooked potatoes to the skillet and cook until they start to brown. Add shallot and garlic, tossing frequently to avoid burning. Add the duck confit and fresh thyme. Toss until the duck is warm all the way through. Deglaze pan with 2 ounces of pheasant stock and reduce by half. If you wish to keep the hash on the crispy side, skip the last step.) Keep warm.

For the Quail Eggs Over Easy

Ingredients

- 4 quail eggs (available at Asian grocers)
- 1 tablespoon clarified butter

Preparation

HEAT the clarified butter in a nonstick skillet. Crack the quail eggs and add to the pan, cooking over medium heat until set. Caution: quail eggs cook very quickly! Do not flip the eggs. If the eggs cook together, separate half of them with a spatula. It makes a nicer presentation if the 2 eggs on each plate are attached.

To Serve "Fowl Play"

PLACE half of the potato hash on the center of each plate. Slice the pheasant breasts thin, on a bias and fan one breast over the hash, covering half of it. Place the 2 quail eggs on the other half of the hash. Sauce about an ounce of the pheasant stock on each plate.

Serves 2

Polenta Crusted Salmon Medallions

Ingredients

4　7-ounce salmon filets cut in half
width-wise
½　cup polenta paste seasoned with
thyme, ginger, salt and white pepper
Chervil/Dill Sauce
Morel mushrooms, quartered

Ramps (or leeks) julienne
Asparagus blanched, extreme bias
julienne
Carrots, julienne finely and blanche
Julienne beet chips (Finely julienne
beets and fry in 300°F oil until crisp)

Chervil/Dill Sauce

½　ounce clarified butter
1　tablespoon shallot, minced
1　teaspoon garlic, minced
1　cup white wine
2　cups heavy cream

2　bay leaves
2　tablespoons chervil, minced
2　tablespoons dill, minced
　　Salt and pepper to taste

Preparation

SAUTÉ shallot in butter until translucent. Add garlic and sauté 30 seconds. Deglaze with wine and reduce demi sec (by half). Add cream and bay leaves and reduce until nappe consistency (coats a spoon). Add herbs and adjust seasoning. Hold in water bath.

IN SMOKING hot skillet, sear salmon medallions on flesh side until nice dore (golden brown). Remove and cool. Coat each salmon medallion with polenta paste and sear polenta side down until polenta crisps and browns. Flip medallions, being careful not to destroy crust, and lightly sear other side. Finish in oven.

IN SAME pan, sauté ramps (or leeks), asparagus, and carrots. Finish with light sauté of mushrooms and cover with sauce.

PLACE Salmon Medallions one on top of the other and spoon Chervil/Dill Sauce ragout around plate. Garnish with julienne beet chips.

Serves 4

HERB AND MUSTARD CRUSTED RACK OF LAMB

Ingredients

4 lamb racks, frenched, fat cap left on
½ cup Panko bread crumbs
1 tablespoon rosemary, minced

1 tablespoon thyme, minced
2 tablespoons Dijon mustard

Preparation

MIX Panko and herbs together. Brush loin with mustard and roll in Panko. Roast in oven at 375°F for 20 minutes or until desired temperature.

Merlot–Thyme Jus

1 ounce clarified butter
3 tablespoons minced shallots
½ bottle merlot
4 sprigs rosemary

1 bunch thyme
2 cups demi-glace
1 cup softened butter

Preparation

SWEAT shallots in butter. Deglaze with merlot and reduce by half. Steep herbs; turn off heat and let sit for 30 minutes. Bring to quick boil, stirring, and add demi-glace. Thicken if necessary with slurry (thin paste of water and cornstarch). Monte au beurre (swirl in softened butter).

Serves 4

Herb and Mustard Crusted Rack of Lamb.

Salad of Red and White Belgian Endive, Roquefort, Toasted Walnuts and Dried Mission Figs

with 30 Year Aged Sherry Vinegar Caramel Sauce

The Caramel Sauce can be made in advance. The amount of vinegar can be adjusted to taste. You can also use your own favorite caramel sauce recipe and deglaze at the end with the sherry vinegar to taste.

Ingredients

> 6 *red endive leaves*
> 6 *white endive leaves*
> ⅓ *cup Roquefort cheese*
> ⅓ *cup walnuts, toasted*

> 4 *dried figs, quartered*
> 3 *ounces Sherry Vinegar Caramel Sauce*
>   *(recipe follows)*
>   *sugar garnish, optional*

Preparation

IN A small bowl, combine the Roquefort, walnuts, figs and 1½ ounces of the Sherry Vinegar Caramel Sauce. Form mixture into 2 rough ball shapes.

For the Sherry Vinegar Caramel Sauce

> ½ *cup granulated sugar*
> ½ *cup water*

> ½ *teaspoon sherry vinegar*
>   *heavy cream (optional)*

PLACE the sugar and water in a small saucepan. Bring to a boil and brush the sides of the pan with a clean brush dipped in water, as necessary. This is to keep any sugar on the sides of the pan from crystallizing. Use only enough water on the brush to achieve this, without letting the extra water drip into the sugar mixture. Cook over medium heat until the sauce reaches a golden amber color. Remove the pan from the heat and carefully add the vinegar; it may splatter. To adjust consistency you can add more water or heavy cream. You can also use the heavy cream to make it a richer sauce, if desired. Let the mixture cool to room temperature before using on the salad.

To Serve

ARRANGE the endive leaves in the pattern of a fan alternating colors, to form a complete circle. There should be 3 of each type of endive on each plate. Place half of the Roquefort mixture on each plate at the base of the fan, in the center of the plate. Spoon the remaining sauce over the endive fans.

GARNISH with a sugar garnish, if desired. Find a basic boiled sugar recipe and make spirals or cages or whatever your preference may be. Place the garnish on top of the Roquefort mixture.

Serves 2

Red
Bird
Restaurant

120 West Front Street
Missoula, MT 59801
406-549-2906

Hours, 5:30 to 9:30 pm
Reservations recommended
Call for directions

Red Bird

Jim Tracey & Laura Waters, Owners
Jim Tracey, Chef

Red Bird opened its doors in November of 1996 with a mission to provide Missoula innovative cuisine using fresh local ingredients. Red Bird is tucked in an alley in the historic Florence Hotel Building and provides intimate evening dining in dramatic architectural surroundings. Husband and wife team, Jim Tracey and Laura Waters, specialize in serving house made pastas, hand cut meats, fresh seafood and delectable desserts. The menu changes seasonally to accommodate the freshest ingredients possible. The ever changing wine list provides boutique style wines with an emphasis on the Northwest region.

The original Florence hotel, built on this site in 1888, offered weary railway travelers and settlers a comfortable night's lodging. The hotel was formerly known as "America's Finest Small Hotel." When it burned in 1913, the Florence was rebuilt as a major 160-room hostelry and was a longtime regional gathering place until it, too, was destroyed by fire in 1936.

Missoula's lack of a major hotel had serious implications, and even though the nation was then in the midst of the depression, Walter H. McLeod and other influential businessmen secured community support to rebuild. When the elegant new Florence Hotel opened in 1941, Spokane Architect G.A. Pehrson masterfully designed the $600,000 "jewel of a hotel" in the new Art Moderne style. Characterized by its rounded corners and horizontal emphasis, terra cotta and glass blocks accent the shiny-smooth concrete and metal surfaces. The splendid 140-room hotel boasted the Northwest's first central air conditioning system, novel glass shower doors and first-class interior appointments in a "harmony of color." One of only two local examples of the style, the third generation Florence reflects the town's steadfast regional importance into the 20th century, the growth of tourism, and the civic pride that prompted its construction.

The Red Bird, a restaurant with new ideas in a historic location, brings back the finest of dining to this historic landmark.

The early Florence Hotel before it burned.

CRAB CAKES WITH MUSTARD EMULSION

Ingredients

¼ cup yellow onion, diced
¼ cup red pepper, diced
1 teaspoon garlic, minced
½ tablespoon butter
16 ounces jumbo lump blue crab meat
2 eggs
¾ cup bread crumbs
½ tablespoon Worcestershire sauce

1 teaspoon Tabasco
¼ teaspoon dry mustard
½ teaspoon salt
½ teaspoon pepper
¼ teaspoon ground cayenne pepper
1 tablespoon parsley, chopped
Mustard Emulsion (recipe follows)

Preparation

SAUTÉ onion, red pepper and garlic in butter in a sauté pan until soft. Scrape the mixture into a bowl, and add all other ingredients except the Mustard Emulsion. Carefully stir the ingredients, making sure not to break crabmeat. Shape small cakes (about ½ cup each) and cook in oil at medium-high heat. Flip crab cakes when edges turn brown.

TO SERVE, place a small pool of mustard emulsion under crab cakes and garnish with fresh herbs and green beans.

Yield 8 crab cakes

For the Mustard Emulsion

1 egg yolk
1 tablespoon white wine vinegar
3 tablespoons Dijon mustard

½ cup chicken stock
1¼ cups olive oil
salt and pepper to taste

BLEND egg, vinegar, mustard, and stock. Continue blending while slowly adding oil. Add salt and pepper to taste.

GRILLED BISON TENDERLOIN
with Red Wine Reduction

Ingredients

4 6-10 oz. bison tenderloin steaks (may
   substitute beef or elk back strap)
2 tablespoons red wine vinegar
1 tablespoon Red Wine Reduction
   (recipe follows)
1 teaspoon dry oregano

1 teaspoon dry basil
1 teaspoon sugar
1 teaspoon pepper
1 teaspoon salt
¼ cup olive oil

WHISK ingredients together and pour over steaks. Marinate for about 1 hour, and then grill steaks to your liking (preferably medium rare). Spoon some of the Red Wine Reduction onto the plate and place the steak on top. Serve with mashed potatoes and oven roasted carrots. At Red Bird we make a crisp potato egg roll.

Serves Four

For the Red Wine Reduction

1 bottle Rippaso wine (Italian red)
¼ cup sugar
   pinch of ground cloves

pinch of ground cinnamon
pinch of salt

REDUCE wine and sugar on low about 40 minutes until it is a syrup consistency. Whisk in clove, cinnamon and salt.

The third Florence Hotel today.

Red Bird, Missoula

DUCK CREPES

Ingredients

¼ cup peanut oil (or olive oil)
1 carrot, shredded
¼ head green cabbage, shredded
1 garlic clove, minced
2 green onions, diced

Shredded Duck (recipe follows)
¼ teaspoon pepper
¼ teaspoon salt
8 Crepes (recipe follows)

Preparation

SEAR vegetables in oil over high heat until the cabbage is wilted. Stir in the shredded duck, salt and pepper. Remove from heat, and place ¼ cup of the mixture in each crepe, then roll like a burrito. Bake for 10 minutes in a 450-degree oven. Serve with a salad, as an appetizer with a soy dipping sauce, or by themselves.

Yield 8 Crepes

For the Shredded Duck

1 green onion
1 star anise
1 slice fresh ginger
2 duck breasts

½ cup soy sauce or tamari
¼ cup water
¼ cup sugar

PLACE all ingredients in a pan and cover. Cook on low for 25 minutes flipping duck occasionally. Remove duck and shred or cut into small pieces.

For the Crepes

½ cup flour
½ cup milk
¼ cup lukewarm water
2 eggs, beaten
2 tablespoons melted butter

½ teaspoon salt
3 tablespoons chives, diced
2 tablespoons black sesame seeds
   butter for cooking

BLEND flour, milk, water, eggs, melted butter, and salt until well combined. Stir in chives and sesame seeds. Cook ¼ cup batter in a 9-inch nonstick pan in a small amount of butter. Flip crepe when edges start to brown. Makes eight crepes.

LOBSTER SOUFFLÉ

Ingredients

5 lobster tails (meat only, raw)
8–10 scallops (medium sized, raw)
1½ tablespoons soft butter

¾ cup Lobster Stock (recipe follows)
1 teaspoon salt
4 egg whites

Preparation

HEAT oven to 350 degrees. Combine lobster, scallops, butter, stock and salt in a food processor and process until smooth. Beat egg whites until soft peaks form. Fold lobster purée and egg whites together carefully trying not to break tiny bubbles in eggs. When combined, fill six individual soufflé dishes half full and bake in a water bath at 350 degrees for about 12 minutes. Soufflés are done when they rise over the top of dish and turn slightly brown. Serve immediately as appetizer or main course.

Serves 6

For the Lobster Stock

2 tablespoons butter
5 lobster shells
½ onion, chopped
½ carrot, chopped
1 cup heavy cream

2 tablespoons cognac or brandy
1 cup white wine
1 teaspoon salt
1 teaspoon pepper

HEAT the butter in a small stockpot. Add the shells, onion, and carrot and cook on medium-high, until carrots are tender and shells are red. Add remaining ingredients, stirring to combine. Cover and simmer about 8–10 minutes. Cool in refrigerator or over an ice bath.

Double Arrow Resort

Highway 83, Mile Marker 12   Hours, 5 p.m. to 9 p.m. daily
Seeley Lake, MT
406–677–2777 or 1–800–468–0777
www.doublearrowresort.com

The Double Arrow Resort

Bryce Finn, Chef

In the late 1920s, Jan Boissevain and Colonel George Wesiel purchased a stock ranch in western Montana, known as the Corbett Ranch. Boissevan, an avid horseman, dreamed of turning this property into a dude ranch, which he would name after the brand on his favorite horse.

His dream became a reality in 1929, when the Double Arrow Ranch was established as the first commercial dude ranch at Seeley Lake. The first couple of years saw major construction of ranch buildings, and the arrival of the first guests, including the president of Cornell University and his wife.

In the fall of 1932, Indians came over the Jocko Pass to camp and hunt on the Double Arrow land. Boissevain felt that they had a right to the continued use of the land and he welcomed them. The Indians never learned to pronounce his name, but nicknamed him "the Bell Boss" after watching him continually ringing the dinner bell. In summer, they often put on their ceremonial costumes and danced for the guests.

Unfortunately, the Great Depression caught up with the recreation business and the Double Arrow struggled to stay afloat. In 1942, he auctioned off the ranch and moved to California. The ranch changed hands several times over the next several decades, sometimes continuing as a dude ranch and sometimes serving as a packing/outfitting headquarters.

In 1989 the lodge was purchased by a group of six couples from the Seattle area, all with Montana roots. Since then, the historic Double Arrow Lodge has undergone significant improvements, while keeping intact its highly valued charm and cozy ambience. All original cabins have been remodeled and upgraded with new lodging units added in the 1990s. A challenging golf course opened in 1994.

Providing a quality dining experience is a commitment of the current owners. Every dish is a culinary treat for the palate and the eye, skillfully prepared from the freshest ingredients by an experienced staff.

 Award of Excellence

Double Arrow Resort, Seeley Lake

Double Arrow Seafood Paella

Ingredients

1   pound of littleneck clams
1   pound of black mussels
2   pounds of peeled and de-veined jumbo prawns
½   pound of sliced andouille sausage
4   3-ounce lobster tails split in half
4   crab claws
2   portabella mushrooms, large dice
½   green onion, chopped

2   tablespoons garlic, chopped
8   cup sun dried tomatoes, julienne
½   cup of fresh Roma tomatoes, diced
2   cups basmati rice
4   cups cold water
2   tablespoons butter
1   tablespoon olive oil
¼   teaspoon saffron
    Salt and pepper to taste

Preparation

IN A medium saucepan bring the 4 cups of water, basmati rice, saffron, and butter to a boil. Add salt and pepper to taste remembering that the fresh seafood will bring its own saltiness to the dish as well. Cover the pan and reduce the heat to low and cook until almost all of the water has been absorbed.

PREHEAT oven to 350°F.

IN A large oven-proof skillet that preferably has a lid, add the olive oil and chopped garlic. Cook the garlic over medium heat until it just begins to brown, add all of the remaining paella ingredients, reserving the Roma tomatoes for the end so as to allow

Seafood Paella.

them to retain as much firmness as possible. Cook all ingredients together in the skillet just until the shrimp begin to turn pink and curl. Add the already hot saffron rice to the skillet and stir all ingredients together. Place the skillet into a preheated 350°F oven and bake for 25 minutes, stirring frequently. When the clams and mussels begin to open the dish is done. Remove from oven and add the Roma tomatoes. Serve in the skillet or plate each portion individually. Serve with your favorite chilled white wine.

Serves 4

ZINFANDEL POACHED PEARS

Ingredients

2 cups white zinfandel wine
½ cup sugar
2 cinnamon sticks
4 Bosc pears
4 cup lemon juice, freshly squeezed
½ cup sour cream

¼ cup Melba Sauce (purchased or homemade)
2 puff pastry sheets
Strawberries (optional for garnish)
Fresh mint

Preparation

PEEL and core the Bosc pears and rub them with freshly squeezed lemon juice so that they do not turn brown before they are poached. In a 2-quart saucepan add the white zinfandel wine, sugar, and cinnamon sticks. Add the peeled pears. Cover the saucepan with tinfoil and place it over a burner on medium heat. Cook the pears until they are fork tender; do not overcook. Remove the pears from the pan and discard the cinnamon sticks. Reduce the sweetened white zinfandel wine over medium heat until it gains the consistency of syrup.

THOROUGHLY chill the poached pears in a refrigerator. Cut the puff pastry sheet length-wise into ½-inch slices. Starting at the bottom of the pear using the puff pastry to plug the whole in the bottom from when it was cored begin to wrap the puff pastry strips around the pear. (You can use your finger dipped in water to help adhere the strips together.) Continue adding strips until you reach the top of the pear. Repeat this with all of the pears. Bake in a preheated 400°F oven until the pears have turned golden brown.

IN A bowl, combine the sour cream and the Melba Sauce together. Using a spoon or pastry bag, fill the hollowed out area of the cored pear with the sauce just before serving. Add a fresh mint sprig to the top, serve with your favorite vanilla ice cream and drizzle with the reduced wine syrup.

MELBA Sauce was created by the famous French chef Auguste Escoffier for Australian opera singer Dame Nellie Melba. To prepare, force 1 cup canned or fresh raspberries through a sieve fine enough to hold back the seeds. Add ¼ cup sugar and cook 6 minutes, or long enough to make a heavy syrup (216°F).

Serves 4

La Provence Restaurant

408 Bridge Street
Bigfork, MT 59911
406-837-2923

Open year-round
Reservations recommended
Deli open, 11:00 am to 2:00 pm
Dining room, 5:30 to 9:00 pm

Marc and Caroline Guizol.

La Provence

Caroline & Marc Guizol, Owners and Chefs

On July 1, 2000, La Provence Restaurant opened its doors to the public, dedicated to bringing a fresh and unique culinary experience to the Flathead Valley of Montana. Nestled in the quaint village of Bigfork, La Provence features French Mediterranean cuisine, prepared with care by Chef Marc Guizol, a native of the south of France and former Dining Room Chef at the Ritz Carlton of Naples, Florida, and Chef at Palace Court Restaurant at Caesars Palace in Las Vegas.

The menu at La Provence changes seasonally. The cuisine features many of the sun-drenched flavors typical of the south of France which have been blended with local products to create a unique fusion of French and Northwestern American flavors. In 2002, La Provence received Wine Spectator Magazine's Best of Award of Excellence for their extensive international wine list, one of only two such awards in Montana.

La Provence features several small dining rooms, decorated with warm colors to create a comfortable and light atmosphere. In addition, a large atrium houses the Wine and Tapes Bar. In 2002 a banquet room, The Lavender Room, was built upstairs from the main restaurant and can seat up to 60 people for private parties and receptions. In the winter months La Provence can seat up to 130 customers in one seating, and in the summer the deck allows an additional 60 outdoor guests. For lunch there is La Petite Provence Deli, daily featuring delicious sandwiches served on French baguettes, homemade soups, fresh salads, and quiche. They have also established a successful full-service catering operation.

La Provence in Bigfork.

About the Owners

Chef Marc was born and raised in a small village in the south of France, right in the heart of Provence. Ever since he was young, he found himself in the kitchen, first helping his mother with the family meals and then in a local restaurant taking the first steps in his career in the food service industry. After working in Italy for a while, Marc returned to France to satisfy his national military duties, serving as personal chef to one of France's top generals. He later moved to England to work at the Four Seasons Inn at the Park Hotel as well as at several world-

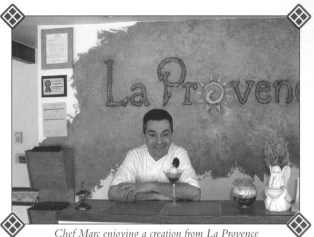

Chef Marc enjoying a creation from La Provence

renowned restaurants in London. After serving as Executive Sous Chef and Acting Executive Chef at the Reids Palace Hotel in Madeira, Portugal, Chef Marc moved to the United States to serve as the Dining Room Chef of the Ritz Carlton Beach Resort in Naples, Florida, where he met his wife-to-be. While at the Ritz, he received the Ivy Award, won a national competition sponsored by Baccardi and Johnson and Whales University and was responsible for the dining room being granted the Mobile Four Star rating and the coveted AAA Five Diamond Award.

From there, Marc took the position as chef at the Palace Court Restaurant at Caesar's Palace in Las Vegas, but soon moved on to Bigfork to turn his dream of owning his own restaurant into a reality.

Caroline grew up in Maryland. After receiving a bachelor's degree in Communications, she then moved on to Johnson and Whales University in Providence, Rhode Island where she graduated Suma Cum Laude with a bachelor's degree in Culinary Arts. After interning with two nationally recognized chefs in New Orleans (John Folse and Greg Sonniers) she worked in the banquet department of the Ritz Carlton in Naples, Florida and at Grey Oaks Country Club in an upscale golf community.

Marc and Caroline Guizol moved to the Flathead Valley early in 2000 with their twin boys, Zachary and Theodore, and their new addition, Nicholas. They currently live in Bigfork.

 Best of Award of Excellence

Parsnip Soup Flavored with Chorizo Sausage

Ingredients

2 tablespoons olive oil
2 pounds parsnips, cut into small cubes
1 onion, chopped
   salt and freshly ground pepper, to taste
2 cups white wine

3 cups cream
1 quart (4 cups) chicken stock
1 bay leaf
8 ounces roasted Chorizo sausage, sliced

Preparation

IN A large stockpot, heat 2 tablespoons olive oil over medium high heat. Add the parsnips and onions. Sauté until the onions are translucent. Season with salt and pepper. Add the white wine and simmer for a few minutes. Add the cream, chicken stock, and bay leaf, stirring to combine. Bring the mixture to a boil, and then reduce heat to low and simmer for 20 minutes.

REMOVE the pot from the stove and puree the soup with a hand blender or in a food processor, working in batches until all the soup has been blended. Run the soup through a chinois and return to the stove. Add the sausage and simmer for 2 minutes more. Check the flavor for salt and pepper, adjust as needed and serve.

Serves 6

Powder River Pool Chalk. Butte county moving from Crow Creek, a tributary of Powder River. (1886)

ROASTED FILLET OF BEEF
with Roquefort Sauce

Ingredients

4 8-ounce Fillet Mignon, seasoned with
   salt and pepper

1 tablespoon olive oil
   Roquefort Sauce (recipe follows)

Preparation

HEAT the oven to 400 degrees. In a heavy bottomed oven-proof skillet, heat the olive oil, then add the seasoned beef fillets. Sear golden brown on all sides and transfer to the hot oven. Cook to desired temperature, then remove from the oven and allow to rest for 5 minutes before serving. Reheat the Roquefort Sauce and serve with the meat.

For the Roquefort Sauce

½ cup onion, chopped
1 tablespoon olive oil
1 cup Chardonnay wine
1 bay leaf
3 cloves
2 tablespoons flour

4 cups chicken stock
2 cups heavy cream
1 cup Roquefort cheese, crumbled
   dash of nutmeg
   salt and pepper to taste

IN A large saucepan, heat the olive oil over medium high heat. Add the onions and sauté until translucent. Add the Chardonnay, bay leaf, and cloves and then bring to a boil. Reduce the heat to a simmer and cook for 2 minutes. Whisk in the flour, then the chicken stock, and then add the cream. Bring back to a boil, stirring frequently. Reduce the heat to low again and gently simmer for 30 minutes, stirring occasionally.

REMOVE the sauce from the heat and pass through a fine strainer. Add the Roquefort cheese to the strained liquid; season to taste with the nutmeg, salt, and pepper. Set aside and keep warm.

Serves 4

Porcini Crème Brûlée

Ingredients

5 egg yolks
1 whole egg
1 cup heavy cream
   salt and pepper to taste
1 cup dried Porcini mushrooms, soaked
   overnight to reconstitute, then
   chopped

2 tablespoons butter
½ cup onions, diced
½ cup white wine
1 teaspoon fresh thyme, chopped
½ cup grated Parmesan cheese

Preparation

HEAT the oven to 275 degrees.

IN A large bowl, combine the eggs, cream, salt and pepper and whisk well to combine. Set aside.

MELT the butter in a medium skillet and add onions and mushrooms. Sauté with salt and pepper and cook for 2 minutes. Add fresh thyme and deglaze the skillet with the white wine. Continue to cook until all of the liquid has evaporated. Remove from heat and allow to cool for 5 minutes.

EVENLY distribute the mushroom mixture among 4 custard cups. Pour the egg mixture evenly into custard cups. To cook the custards evenly, you need to prepare a Bain Marie. Place the custard cups in a 2-inch deep baking dish, transfer to the oven and carefully pour warm water into the baking dish so that the cups are sitting in a warm bath of water. Cook until the custard is just set without browning the top – approximately 30 minutes.

REMOVE from the oven and set aside to cool for a few minutes. Sprinkle the tops with the grated Parmesan cheese and place under a broiler until the cheese becomes golden brown. Remove from the broiler and serve immediately.

Serves 4

Rack of Lamb
With Provençal Salsa Sauce

For the Lamb

2 tablespoons cooking oil
2 racks of lamb

Salt and pepper to taste

For the Provençal Salsa

1 cup diced tomatoes
2 tablespoons pesto

1 sprig fresh rosemary, chopped
¼ cup Kalamata olives, chopped

Preparation for the Salsa

COMBINE all the ingredients in a small mixing bowl and allow the flavors to steep at room temperature for at least 1 hour. Cover and refrigerate until ready to use.

For the Wine Sauce

2 cups beef brown sauce, simmered to reduce to 1 cup
1½ cups red wine (a burgundy), simmered to reduce to 2 cup

Salt and pepper to taste
Optional herbs, such as Herbs de Provençe or fresh rosemary

COMBINE the reduced brown sauce and reduced wine. Continue simmering to combine flavors and reduce slightly. Add salt and pepper and herbs to taste. (This is called a "traditional wine sauce.")

THEN mix one cup of the traditional wine sauce with 4 tablespoons of the prepared Provençal Salsa.

Preparation

PREHEAT oven to 375°.

SEASON the lamb with salt and pepper. In a large skillet over medium-high heat, sear the racks on all sides. Remove the skillet from the stove and transfer to the oven. Cook for approximately 10 minutes or until desired internal temperature is achieved. Remove the racks from the oven and allow to rest on a cutting board in a warm place for 10 minutes. In a small saucepan heat the red wine sauce to a boil. Add the salsa and simmer for a few minutes. Adjust the seasoning with salt and pepper as desired and set aside.

WHEN ready to serve, portion the racks by slicing between the rib bones and arrange on serving plates. Spoon the sauce over the lamb and serve immediately. You can accompany this dish with seasonal vegetables and potato gratin.

CHERRY CLAFOUTI

The cherries need to be marinated at least 24 hours before you prepare the dessert.

Ingredients

30 *fresh Bing cherries, pitted and marinated in Chambord*
2 *cups heavy cream*
7 *eggs*

1 *cup granulated sugar*
1 *teaspoon vanilla extract*
powdered sugar for dusting
vanilla ice cream

Preparation

HEAT the oven to 350 degrees. To prepare the baking dishes you will need individual ovenproof brulee dishes. Butter the dishes and place 5 marinated cherries in each dish. Set aside.

IN A large mixing bowl, blend the cream, eggs, sugar and vanilla with a wire whisk. Pour the mixture evenly over the cherries in each baking dish. Place the dishes in the oven. Cook until the clafouti is just set and the cherries have just begun putting off their juices on the surface. Remove from oven and allow to cool slightly.

TO SERVE, dust the warm clafouti with powdered sugar, and top with a small scoop of vanilla ice cream.

Serves 6

Cafe Max

121 Main Street
Kalispell, MT 59901
406-755-7687
www.cafemaxmontana.com

Open for Dinner
Tuesday–Saturday 5:30 pm
Reservations recommended

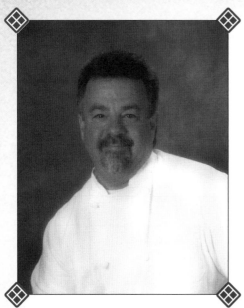

Cafe Max

Douglas and Vonnie Day, Owners
Douglas Day, Chef

Cafe Max is located in historic downtown Kalispell. Chef Doug Day earned his culinary degree from Johnson and Wales University in Providence, Rhode Island, and worked in some of the country's most notable restaurants in Florida, the Virgin Islands, and Seattle before opening Cafe Max in 1996. The restaurant is renowned for inventive cuisine and professional service. Chef Day was voted "Best Chef in the Flathead Valley" and Cafe Max "The Flathead Valley's Best Fine Dining Restaurant, since 2001."

The menus at Cafe Max change frequently to follow the elements of the seasons, emphasizing ingredients from the Pacific Northwest. Seafood dishes are prepared with king salmon, halibut, and ocean scallops from the cold, clear waters of Alaska.

Menus include premium Angus beef, lamb, veal, chicken, and vegan entrées, as well as an extensive selection of wines and fabulous desserts. In keeping with the philosophy of the dinner menus, the wine list is an eclectic selection from around the world with an emphasis on the wines of Washington and Oregon. Cafe Max frequently hosts popular six-course wine dinners and more casual evenings of food and winetasting, which include discussions of each wine and the food with which it is paired.

 Award of Excellence

Chef Doug Day invites anyone with questions about Cafe Max recipes to email him:
chezday@centurytel.net.

CHICKEN CROQUETTE STUFFED
with Wild Mushroom Risotto

Ingredients

1 single lobe chicken breast, 6 to 8 ounces
  chopped fresh parsley
  salt and pepper to taste
2–3 ounces Wild Mushroom Risotto (Recipe follows)

flour
1 egg, lightly beaten to make an egg wash
  bread crumbs
  olive oil for sautéing

Preparation

BUTTERFLY the chicken breast and place between two pieces of plastic wrap. With a small meat mallet, pound lightly to reduce to ¼ inch thickness. Remove top piece of plastic and shape breast into a rectangle. Season with salt, pepper, and parsley.

PLACE 2 to 3 ounces of the Wild Mushroom Risotto at the bottom edge of the flattened breast. Roll forward, creating a cylinder, ending with the seam side down. Reshape to minimize any uneven edges. Wrap in bottom layer of plastic wrap and refrigerate for 20 minutes.

HEAT oven to 350 degrees. Unwrap the cylinder and carefully dredge with flour, not letting it unroll. Dip in egg wash and then roll in breadcrumbs. Secure with toothpicks, if necessary.

SAUTÉ in ½ inch olive oil, browning on all sides. Remove to a shallow pan and finish in a 350-degree oven for approximately 15 to 20 minutes. Remove from oven; let rest for 3 to 4 minutes, and then slice.

IF PREFERRED, you can drizzle a sauce, such as marinara, alfredo, or béchamel over the slices before serving.

Serves 1

WILD MUSHROOM RISOTTO

Ingredients

1½ pounds mixed wild mushrooms, such as chanterelles, shiitakes, pine mushrooms

¼ cup olive oil, divided

4–5 garlic cloves, finely chopped and divided in half

salt and pepper to taste

2 cups chicken stock, heated

2 tablespoons unsalted butter, divided

1 onion, chopped

1½ cups Arborio rice

1 cup freshly grated Parmesan cheese

1 bunch Italian parsley, stems removed and finely chopped

Preparation

REMOVE bases on the stems of the mushrooms. Wash mushrooms in cold water and dry in a salad spinner. Chop coarsely.

IN A heavy saucepan, heat 3 tablespoons of the olive oil. Add the mushrooms a little at a time. Sauté briefly and then add half the chopped garlic. Season with salt and pepper, and sauté for a couple of minutes more. Keep warm.

IN ANOTHER heavy pan, heat 1 tablespoon of the butter with the rest of the olive oil. Add the chopped onion and cook on low heat until the onion is transparent. Add the remaining chopped garlic and cook for a minute. Add the rice, stirring until each grain is coated.

SLOWLY start ladling in the heated stock, constantly stirring. Allow each ladleful of stock to be absorbed by the rice before adding more. Continue until the rice is cooked al dente, usually about 20 minutes.

ADD the cooked wild mushrooms, the remaining tablespoon of butter and the chopped Italian parsley, stirring to combine.

Serves 6

BREAST OF DUCK WITH FLATHEAD CHERRY SAUCE

Ingredients

4 boned duck breast halves
3 tablespoons butter
2½ tablespoons sugar
2 Macintosh apples, peeled, cored, and chopped
2 cups syrah or cabernet sauvignon
2 pounds (about 4 cups) fresh Flathead cherries, pitted (can use any sweet cherries)

⅛ teaspoon cinnamon
4 whole cloves
¼ teaspoon nutmeg
Salt and pepper
1 cup water

Preparation

MELT sugar in 2 tablespoons butter in a large skillet over medium heat. Turn heat to medium-high, add apples and cook, stirring frequently until softened and browned, about 8 minutes. Add red wine and reduce for 4 minutes.

LOWER heat to medium, add 1 cup water, 3 cups cherries, cinnamon, cloves, and nutmeg. Season with salt and pepper. Mash cherries with a wooden spoon, then simmer mixture until liquid is reduced by half, 15-20 minutes.

STRAIN sauce through a fine sieve, then return to skillet. Add remaining cherries and simmer over medium heat until sauce has reduced by a third, about 8 minutes. Reduce heat to low.

SCORE the fat side of the duck breasts and season both sides with salt and pepper. Heat a large skillet over medium heat. Add duck breasts with the fat side down and cook until the skin is crisp, about 12 minutes. Pour off excess fat. Turn and continue cooking for 6 to 8 minutes more.

REMOVE duck from skillet and slice thin. Whisk remaining 1 tablespoon butter into sauce and spoon over duck.

APPLEWOOD SMOKED TENDERLOIN OF BUFFALO
with Horseradish Caper Cream

Ingredients

3 5-ounce medallions of buffalo
tenderloin
Salt and pepper

1 tablespoon butter
Vine-ripened tomato slices

SEASON medallions with salt and pepper, then sear in butter until browned on both sides, about 5 minutes. Place in heated smoker with applewood chips for 10 minutes, remove and chill.

Horseradish Caper Cream

2 tablespoons horseradish
2 tablespoons whipped cream
1 teaspoon lemon juice

1 tablespoon wild capers
Salt

MIX first four ingredients together and add salt to taste.

SERVE Smoked Buffalo Tenderloins with sliced vine-ripened tomatoes and Horseradish Caper Cream.

Painted Horse Grille

110 Main Street
Kalispell, MT 59901
Hotel Reservations 1-800-858-7422
406-257-7035 or 406-755-8100
grand@kalispellgrand.com
www.paintedhorsegrille.com

Dinner served Monday-Saturday
5:30 – 9:00 p.m.
Lunch served Monday-Friday

Charbroiled Buffalo Striploin.

The Painted Horse Grille
in the Kalispell Grand

C. M. & Janet Clark, Owners
Brett Morris, Chef

The Kalispell Grand Hotel offers historic accommodations and fine dining for the discerning traveler in the Painted Horse Grille, all just 30 minutes from Glacier National Park in Montana's magnificent Flathead Valley.

From the inception of the frontier hotel business, this hotel was known for its finer amenities. In 1912, the Kalispell Hotel hosted the relatively well-to-do traveller at a charge of $2 per night. This was considered twice the going rate of other hotels at that time. However, being situated in the heart of Kalispell's downtown business district and offering such privileged services as running water, door locks, and wake-ups, the Kalispell Hotel rarely hung out its vacancy sign.

The three-story brick structure, designed by Kalispell architect Marion Riffo and built by local contractor B. Brice Gilliland, has stood through the years as a silent sentinel to the changes in the Flathead Valley and downtown Kalispell. During World War I, information about the war was shouted to crowds of people at the corner of First and Main. In 1919, the City of Kalispell installed a water fountain on the corner where the hotel still stands, emphasizing the importance of the First and Main intersection. On weekend nights, the Opera House crowd would gather around the fountain and frequent the hotel lobby. Several patrons would eventually stay the night.

Famed western artist Charlie Russell was a good friend of Frank Bird Linderman, a noted writer who leased and managed the hotel from 1924 to 1926. Linderman, Russell, and author Irvin S. Cobb were close friends and on occasion took lunch together and then would saunter back to the hotel lobby's stuffed leather chairs. Here they would sit and exchange thoughts and stories of the West. Linderman, who lived the life of a

The Kalispell Grand today.

Painted Horse Grille, Kalispell

true plainsman, migrated up the Missouri, and continued overland to settle in Kalispell. He later wrote books and novels that are still eagerly sought after by book collectors across the country. Charlie Russell's work is world-renowned, and found only in the finest art galleries today.

The Kalispell Grand in the 1920s.

Through the years, a number of individuals have owned the hotel. At one point in the 1930s, the owners planned extensive renovations, including the addition of a fourth floor and what would have been Kalispell's first passenger elevator. These renovations never occurred; however, between 1939 and 1941 the interior of the Kalispell Hotel was remodeled. According to a contemporary newspaper description:

" . . . The modern hotel room of today has to be definitely different than that of some few years ago, as most of the travelling public of today carry radios and electric razors in its luggage, and demands box springs and inner spring mattresses for sleeping comfort. An entirely new plan of interior decoration has been carried out that is highly attractive to the eyes and gives the guest who steps within its hospitable doors and immediate feeling of physical well being and luxury as well as appealing to his aesthetic sense."

After early prosperity, the hotel fell on hard times during more recent decades and was reduced to taking in weekly, monthly, and even hourly tenants.

But in 1989, a major renovation began that brought the hotel back to vibrant life. The 51 "bath down the hall" rooms that had rented for $120 to $150 per month were transformed into 40 rooms with private baths, furnished in Victorian-style cherry wood.

The hotel reopened to guests in 1991 while renovation of the lobby continued. Today, the sweep of the original lobby can be seen, including the original oak stairway and the high, pressed-tin ceiling.

Early in Kalispell's history, there were eight downtown hotels, and today, only one remains—the Kalispell Grand Hotel. Inside the gracious lobby, guests can still envision the life and history of a bygone era. The Kalispell Grand Hotel is a living landmark in downtown Kalispell.

The hotel's restaurant, The Painted Horse Grille, offers some of the finest dining in the Flathead Valley. In its casual, upscale atmosphere, Chef Brett Morris prepares his creative dinner cuisine, including pasta entrées, succulent steaks, roasted pine nut encrusted salmon, rosemary-lingonberry rack of lamb, and Indian curry spiced duck breast. For lunch experience a variety of fresh salads, homemade soups, paella, and an array of homemade baguette sandwiches. Creatively prepared lunch and dinner specials are offered every day. Exquisite desserts, an extensive and well-selected wine list, and a full liquor selection complement your dining experience.

FILLET OF BEEF
with Portobello Mushroom Brandy Demi Glace

Ingredients

4 8-ounce fillets of beef
   olive oil
¼ cup onion, diced
1 tablespoon garlic, chopped
1 cup brandy
1 sprig fresh rosemary

1 cup demi glace
4 Portobello mushrooms, stems and gills
   removed and sliced
   corn starch mixed in cold water, for
   thickening
   salt and pepper to taste

Preparation

IN A 12" to 14" sauté pan, sauté onion and garlic in a little olive oil until tender. Carefully add brandy and flame. When flame dies down, add rosemary and reduce volume by one half. Strain through a fine mesh sieve into another large sauté pan and add demi glace.

IN A separate sauté pan, sauté the mushrooms lightly in olive oil and add to sauce. Bring mixture to a boil and reduce sauce by one half. Whisk in corn starch mixed with cold water, a little at a time, until the desired thickness is achieved. Adjust flavor with salt and pepper to taste. Set aside and keep warm.

COOK fillets to desired temperature on preheated grill.

TO SERVE, place a little sauce on each plate and set fillets on top of sauce. Ladle additional sauce over each fillet. Serve with mashed or roasted potatoes and a green salad.

Serves 4

Charbroiled Buffalo Striploin
with Brandy Morel Mushroom Cream Sauce

The Buffalo Striploin complemented with a Brandy Morel Cream Sauce is one of our most popular special entrées. Our guests sing praises of the tenderness and taste.

For the Meat

Prepare a hot grill
4 *8-ounce buffalo strip steaks lightly seasoned with salt and pepper*

For the Brandy Morel Mushroom Cream Sauce

3-4 *tablespoons butter*
¼ *cup chopped onion*
2 *teaspoons chopped garlic*
½-1 *cup chopped or sliced fresh morel mushrooms (dried morels re-hydrated in warm water and drained and sliced may be used)*

½ *cup brandy*
1 *cup demi-glace or rich brown stock*
1 *cup heavy cream*
Salt and pepper to taste
Roux, if needed (a mixture of flour and fat used as a thickening agent)

Preparation

PREPARE sauce first and keep warm while broiling steaks.

PLACE buffalo over hot coals or gas grill and broil until desired temperature (medium rare is suggested).

SAUTÉ onion, garlic, and mushrooms in butter in a saucepan or large skillet until browned. Remove from heat and add brandy. Place back on burner and flame, burning off the alcohol. When flame subsides add demi-glace or stock, bring to a boil and reduce one-half to one-third volume.

ADD heavy cream and reduce by boiling till desired thickness is reached. Add salt and pepper to taste. If you are preparing sauce ahead of time, whisk in a little roux to keep sauce from breaking up.

Serves 4

TRIPLE CHOCOLATE PECAN TORTE

Ingredients

14 ounces dark bittersweet chocolate
½ cup unsalted butter
1 cup whipping cream
5 eggs
½ cup sugar
1 teaspoon vanilla extract

2 cups pecan pieces, finely ground in a
food processor
Chocolate Butter Cream (recipe
follows)
Chocolate Glaze (recipe follows

Preparation

HEAT oven to 325 degrees. Line bottom of a spring form pan with parchment. Rub the parchment and the sides of the pan with a little softened butter, and dust lightly with flour.

PLACE the chocolate, butter, and cream in a saucepan over low heat, until the chocolate is melted. Stir occasionally until the mixture is thoroughly combined and smooth.

PLACE the eggs, sugar, and vanilla in a 5-1/2 quart mixing bowl. Bring a saucepan of water to a simmer, and place the mixing bowl in the saucepan so that the bottom of the bowl comes in contact with the simmering water. Whisk the mixture with a wire whip over the simmering water until the mixture is warm. Remove the bowl from the water and place it on a mixer. Using the wire whip beat the mixture on high speed until it triples in volume.

FOLD the ground nuts into the melted chocolate mixture. Then carefully fold the egg mixture into the chocolate nut mixture. Pour the batter into the prepared spring form pan and cover sides of the pan with foil. Place pan in a water bath and bake 40 to 45 minutes in a 325-degree oven, or until a toothpick comes out clean when placed in center of cake.

PLACE cake on a cooling rack and remove foil from pan. Let cool to room temperature.

WHEN cool, remove cake from pan. Using a narrow icing spatula dipped in warm water, spread the Chocolate Butter Cream on top and sides of the cake. Note: you may cut cake in half crosswise and ice the middle, if desired.

CHILL cake in refrigerator until the butter cream is set up. Then smooth top and sides of cake with a hot wet spatula. Pour Chocolate Glaze over top of cake and gently spread the sides with a spatula. Refrigerate until glaze is hard.

Yield 1 torte

For the Chocolate Butter Cream

    6 ounces dark bittersweet chocolate,
      melted
    6 egg yolks
    ½ cup granulated sugar

    ½ cup whipping cream
    1 pound unsalted butter
    ¼ cup crème de cocoa
    5 cups powdered sugar

IN A mixing bowl, whisk the egg yolks into the melted chocolate, then whisk in the granulated sugar and whipping cream. Place mixing bowl over simmering water and whisk until mixture forms a medium custard, about 10 to 15 minutes. Remove from water and let cool to room temperature.

BEAT butter in a 5½ quart mixing bowl until creamy. Gradually beat in chocolate custard mixture, and then add crème de cocoa. Gradually beat in the powdered sugar.

Yield: enough for 2 tortes

For the Chocolate Gaze

    6 ounces dark bittersweet chocolate
    6 ounces butter

    3 tablespoons corn starch

PLACE all ingredients in a small saucepan over low heat and cook, stirring constantly, until mixture is melted and totally blended together. Set aside.

Yield: enough for 1 torte

LEMON MASCARPONE CHEESECAKE
with Black Raspberry Sauce

Crust Ingredients

1 cup graham cracker crumbs
¼ cup sugar

⅓ cup melted butter
Zest of 1 lemon

To Prepare Crust

PREHEAT oven to 350°F.

MIX graham cracker crumbs, sugar, and lemon zest together, add melted butter, mix until moist. Press in bottom of ungreased 9-inch springform pan. Bake for 10 minutes at 350°F.

COOL on rack while cheesecake batter is being prepared. Wrap springform pan bottom with foil before baking in water bath.

Cheesecake Ingredients

3 8-ounce packages cream cheese, softened
1 cup mascarpone cheese
1 cup sugar
2 eggs

1 fresh lemon, including zest (4 tablespoons juice)
4 tablespoons flour
1 tablespoon vanilla

To Prepare Cheesecake Filling

PREHEAT oven to 350°F.

BLEND cream cheese with electric mixer until soft, add sugar, mascarpone, zest of 1 lemon, lemon juice, and vanilla. Mix until all ingredients are well-combined and smooth. Add eggs one at a time on low speed just until mixed in (about ½ minute). Stir in flour by hand. Do not overmix.

POUR the batter into prebaked graham cracker crust (with foil-wrapped bottom). Bake in preheated oven in water bath (shallow pan with about 1 to 2 inches of water) for 1 hour. Turn oven off and let stand for 30 minutes with oven door closed.

Black Raspberry Sauce

COMBINE 1 quart fresh or frozen black raspberries with 1 cup of sugar in a stainless steel bowl and leave at room temperature. Pass thawed ingredients through a food mill until seeds are removed, leaving a thick, smooth sauce.

To Serve

CUT in cheesecake wedges and spoon black raspberry sauce over.

Corner House Grille

147 Central Ave.
Whitefish, MT 59937
406-863-2323

Call for reservations
Dinner served nightly from 5:00 p.m.
Closed Tuesday

Corner House Grille
Zachary Bernheim, Chef

For an evening of rustic elegance, The Corner House Grille is the perfect choice. It is located on the corner of 2nd and Central Avenue in downtown Whitefish, at the base of Big Mountain Ski Resort. The interior sports brick walls, gleaming wood floors, and large wood-framed mirrors that reflect the elegant table service of white linen. Massive carriage lanterns create a soft glow as you enjoy your meal, and the open kitchen lets you get a peak at the action, as your food is expertly prepared.

Chef Zachary Bernheim has created a wonderful menu of New American cuisine that emphasizes bold colors and flavors utilizing organic meats, fish, and vegetables presented at their seasonal best. Chef Zach began cooking professionally in Boulder, Colorado at the tender age of 13. He has since worked for many well-known chefs, including Michel Richard (Citrus, Citronelle) and Wolfgang Puck (Spago, Granita, Chinois). Cooking for more than twenty years from Hawaii to New Orleans, Chef Zach has gleaned the best from each position he filled, learning ideas about presentation and seasonality at one place, while learning about flavors and technique at others. These twenty years of culinary experience have culminated in the innovative menu of the Corner House Grille.

The wine list is heavily laden with many hard-to-find boutique labels, and showcases more than twenty-five wines by the glass, giving the adventurous wine lover a chance to try many new wines.

There is something to please every taste on the "melting pot" menu, from Asian-inspired dishes to Pacific Northwest flavors to the all-American steaks and wild game dishes. After a day of skiing the Big Mountain or hiking in the National Forests surrounding Whitefish, a luxurious meal prepared and hospitably served by the professional wait staff will cap a perfect day in northwest Montana.

Corner House Grille, Whitefish

176

FRENCH ONION SOUP IN AN ONION SHELL

Ingredients

8 large yellow onions
   heavily salted ice water
8 shallots, peeled and thinly sliced
1 garlic bulb, peeled and thinly sliced
½ cup olive oil
4 tablespoons unsalted butter
1 tablespoon fresh thyme
1 cup soy sauce

1 cup sherry wine
12 cups chicken stock
   salt and pepper to taste
8 large croutons made from French
   baguette bread
8 1-ounce slices Provolone cheese
8 1-ounce slices Gruyere or Swiss
   cheese

Preparation

CUT ⅓ off the bottom, root end, of each of the onions. Gently pull the inside layers out of the large portion of each onion, leaving 2 to 3 outer layers of the bulb intact. Submerge the onion "shells" in heavily salted ice water and store them in the refrigerator for a minimum of 6 hours or up to 24 hours.

SLICE the onions that you have scooped out into very thin slices. Over high heat, in a stockpot, caramelize the onions in olive oil and butter until dark brown. Add the thyme and deglaze the pan with the soy and sherry wine. Add the chicken stock and bring the mixture to a boil. Reduce the heat and simmer for 30 to 60 minutes. The finished product should be equal parts of broth and onion. Adjust the seasoning if necessary with salt and pepper.

JUST before serving, remove the onion shells from the salted water, rinse, and place on a sheet tray. Preheat the broiler on high. Fill the onion shells with the hot soup. Drop a crouton into each "bowl" and drape the Provolone and then the Swiss cheese slices over them. Put the whole tray under the preheated broiler to brown the cheese. The combination of the hot soup and the intense heat of the broiler should cook the onion shells enough to make them just soft enough to eat. If you would like them to be cooked a little more, brush them with olive oil and bake them for 3 to 4 minutes in a 350-degree oven before filling them with the soup.

PLACE each soup-filled onion in a bowl and serve with additional French bread.

Serves 8

GINGER SPIKED AHI TUNA SAIMIN STYLE

Ingredients

4 Ahi Tuna fillets
4 tablespoons fresh ginger, grated
1 teaspoon crushed red chilies
1 teaspoon Kosher or sea salt
1 teaspoon coarse black pepper
  sesame oil
  olive or canola oil
  Soy Broth (recipe follows)
8 prawns, peeled and deveined
1 red bell pepper, julienned

1 yellow bell pepper, julienned
1 bunch green onions, cut in 3-inch
  segments
8 shiitake mushrooms, stems removed
1 celery rib, cut crosswise on a bias
½ pound broccoli florettes
8 ounces bamboo shoots
8 ounces water chestnuts
2 pounds Yakisoba noodles (or ramen)

For the Soy Broth

3 tablespoons fresh ginger, chopped
2 limes, juiced
½ cup soy sauce
2 teaspoons finely ground black pepper

1 jalapeno, seeded and chopped
3 cups chicken stock
3 cups water
2 tablespoons sesame oil

PLACE all the ingredients in a large non-reactive sauce pan and bring to a boil. Reduce the heat and simmer for about 20 minutes. Strain the broth and keep warm.

Preparation

GENEROUSLY coat the fish on one side with the grated ginger, red chilies, salt, and pepper. Cover and refrigerate.

POUR sesame oil and olive or canola oil in a 50/50 ratio into a skillet to a ¼ inch depth. Heat the oil and sauté the fish until the desired doneness. Do not overcook. Tuna should be rare inside. Remove tuna and keep warm.

IN A large pot, bring the Soy Broth to a boil; add the prawns and bring back to a boil. In rapid succession, add the cut vegetables to the boiling liquid in the order stated above. Allow the liquid to come back to a complete boil before adding the noodles. Continue to cook for 1 minute.

TO SERVE, divide the broth, vegetables, and noodles into 4 large bowls. Place 1 piece of tuna on top of each one. Serve immediately.

Serves 4

Five Spiced Duck Breast
with Green Vegetables and Chinese Mustard Jus

Ingredients

4 boneless duck breasts
4 teaspoons five-spice powder
1 tablespoon Kosher salt
2 tablespoons sesame oil
1 napa cabbage, outer leaves removed
    and quartered

4 baby bok choy
12 snow peas, deribbed
1 cup Chinese Mustard Jus (recipe
    follows)

Preparation

LIGHTLY score the skin of the duck breasts with a sharp knife. Rub each breast with 1 teaspoon of the five-spice powder and a pinch of Kosher salt. Allow the duck to sit at room temperature for a few minutes.

IN A large sauté pan over medium high heat, add the sesame oil and sauté the seasoned duck breasts skin side down for approximately 7 minutes. Turn the duck over and cook an additional 5 to 10 minutes to your preferred doneness. Remove from pan and keep warm.

POUR off all but a few tablespoons of the fat rendered from the duck breast. Add the cabbage, bok choy, and snow peas to the pan and sauté them for about 2 minutes. Add 1 cup of the Chinese Mustard Jus and cook for about 1 more minute.

TO SERVE, divide the vegetables evenly and place in the center of four plates. Slice the duck breasts on a slight bias and fan the slices in a half moon up against the vegetables. Spoon 2 ounces of the sauce over the vegetables and serve.

Serves 4

For the Chinese Mustard Jus

2 tablespoons sesame oil
1 tablespoon canola or vegetable oil
2 tablespoons fresh ginger, minced
2 tablespoons hot Chinese mustard
    powder

1 tablespoon garlic, crushed
4 cups chicken stock
2 ounces soy sauce
1 tablespoon honey

PUT the oils, ginger, and garlic into a cold saucepan and place over medium heat. Gently sauté for 2 to 3 minutes. Mix the mustard powder with ½ cup of the chicken stock and add to the pan along with the soy sauce and honey. Quickly whisk in the remaining stock and simmer until reduced to 3 cups.

Yield 3 cups

GRILLED TUSCAN RIBEYES

with Parmesan Grilled Polenta and Roasted Onions

Ingredients

4 ribeye steaks
4 tablespoons garlic, sliced and
   blanched
1 jalapeno, seeded and minced
6 ounces sun-dried tomato,
   reconstituted in water until soft
2 ounces fresh oregano
1 bunch Italian parsley, chopped

1 teaspoon Kosher or sea salt
1 teaspoon crushed red chilies
1 teaspoon coarse black pepper
4 ounces extra virgin olive oil
   Parmesan Grilled Polenta (recipe
   follows)
   Roasted Onions (recipe follows)

Preparation

TOSS the garlic, jalapeno, sun-dried tomato, herbs, and spices together with the olive oil until combined. Generously coat the ribeyes with the mixture, wrap tightly and refrigerate.

ON A medium hot grill, place the Roasted Onion packets over the hottest part and arrange the steaks around them. Cook the steaks half way through without turning or moving them. Then move the onion packets and steaks to either a cooler part of the grill or to the top level, if available, and close the lid.

WHEN the steaks are nearly finished, place the polenta, oiled side down, over the hottest part of the grill to mark them. Cook them only on this side or you run the risk of them sticking to the grill.

TO SERVE, place one section of the grilled polenta, marked side up, on each plate. Place one of the grilled ribeyes on top of the polenta. Cut open the foil pouches with the onions, and deposit their contents on top of each steak.

Serves 4

For the Parmesan Grilled Polenta

4 cups chicken stock or water
2 tablespoons butter
2 cups polenta
2 teaspoons finely ground black pepper

1 cup Parmesan cheese, grated
1 teaspoon Kosher salt
2 ounces olive oil

BRING the stock or water, butter, and salt to a boil. Add the polenta and reduce to a simmer. Continue cooking, stirring constantly, until most of the liquid is absorbed. Quickly mix in the pepper, Parmesan cheese and salt, and transfer the polenta to a lightly greased sheet pan or shallow baking dish. Smooth the mixture into one uniform thickness and refrigerate. Once cool, remove the polenta from the pan by running a thin knife around the edge of the pan, then inverting the whole on to a cutting board. Flip polenta back over so that the right side is up and brush the top with olive oil. Cut into 4 equal portions and hold in the refrigerator.

For the Roasted Onions

1 *small red onion, quartered*	2 *ounces extra virgin olive oil*
1 *small yellow onion, quartered*	1 *ounce red wine vinegar*
4 *shallots*	1 *teaspoon Kosher salt*
4 *garlic cloves*	1 *teaspoon black pepper*

TOSS all ingredients in a bowl to coat and season them evenly. Separate into 4 equal portions and wrap each portion loosely in aluminum foil. Set aside until ready to put on the grill.

Charles M. Russell and his horse "Monte" early 1880's.

HERB GRILLED KING SALMON
with Fire Roasted Lemon Potatoes and Pepper Slaw

Although this is not the kind of cooking we normally do at the Corner House Grille, I have included it because it is the type of thing I love to cook at home. All the prep is done in advance and can all be cooked on the grill for minimal cleanup. It is perfect for dinner on a hot summer day when you have guests in town and have spent the day either in Glacier National Park or at the beach.

Ingredients

4 king salmon fillets
1 bunch parsley
1 tablespoon fresh thyme leaves
1 tablespoon sage
1 teaspoon Kosher salt

1 teaspoon black pepper
2 ounces olive oil
Fire Roasted Lemon Potatoes (recipe follows)
Pepper Slaw (recipe follows)

Preparation

CHOP the herbs as finely as you can and mix them with the olive oil, salt, and pepper to form a thick herb "salad". Coat the fish on all sides with this mixture; cover and refrigerate until service.

START the grill about 45 minutes before service, and remove the coated salmon fillets, the Fire Roasted Lemon Potatoes, and the Pepper Slaw from the refrigerator so that they can come to room temperature. Set a colander over a bowl and put the potato mixture in it to drain, reserving the liquid.

PLACE the salmon on the outside coolest part of the grill and arrange the drained potatoes in a single layer over the hotter area. Allow the potatoes to brown before moving. The fish should cook for 3 to 5 minutes on each side, depending on the heat of the grill.

WHEN the salmon fillets are cooked and the potatoes are browned, remove them from the grill. Serve family style on one large platter. Arrange the fillets and the potatoes in a ring around the edge of the platter. Pour the reserved marinade from the potatoes over both the fish and potatoes. Mound the slaw in the center of the platter.

Serves 4

For the Fire Roasted Lemon Potatoes

2 pounds Yukon gold or other waxy
    potatoes
½ cup olive oil
2 lemons, juiced

2 teaspoons Kosher salt
2 teaspoons finely ground black pepper
½ teaspoon crushed red chilies

THINLY slice the potatoes into ¼ inch thick rounds and place in a plastic zipper bag along with the olive oil, lemon juice, salt, pepper, and crushed chilies. Remove as much air as possible and refrigerate until about 45 minutes before serving.

For the Pepper Slaw

1 red bell pepper
1 yellow bell pepper
1 small red onion
3 tablespoons red wine vinegar

1 tablespoon olive oil
2 teaspoons sugar
    salt and pepper to taste

CUT the peppers in half and remove seeds and ribs; julienne them lengthwise as thin as possible. Cut the onion in half, removing the outside paper layer, and then cutting very thin strips in a radius from end to end. Combine the oil, vinegar, and sugar in a plastic zipper bag, seal and shake to combine. Add the peppers and onion, seal, and shake again. Refrigerate until about 45 minutes before serving.

General Sheridan and party at Old Faithful. Old Faithful spouting in background. (1881)

FRESH ELK HAM
with Wild Morels and Red Wine Risotto

I love this recipe because nearly everyone in Montana hunts and they all seem to eat the quickest parts first, leaving the less readily available pieces for last. With the spring morel rush in the Flathead, the elk ham that you got in the fall of last year may very well still be in the deep freeze when the first mushrooms pop out.

You will want to start this recipe the day before you are serving it, letting the juices of the broth penetrate back into the meat as it cools overnight.

Ingredients

4–6 *pound elk ham, uncooked & uncured*
1 *teaspoon juniper berries*
2 *tablespoons black peppercorns*
1 *tablespoon white peppercorns*
1 *tablespoon Kosher salt*
1 *teaspoon cloves*
1 *teaspoon thyme*

1 *tablespoon sage*
1 *large carrot*
2 *celery ribs*
1 *small onion*
2 *tablespoons honey*
  Red Wine Risotto (recipe follows)
  Wild Morels (recipe follows)

THE day before serving, heat the oven to 250 degrees. Place the elk ham, spices, herbs, and vegetables in a large pot, along with the honey. Fill the pot with water to cover the mixture. Bring the mixture to a gentle simmer and transfer to the 250-degree oven for 2 hours. Remove from oven and cool in an ice bath or, preferably, place in refrigerator to cool overnight.

ON THE day of service, heat the oven to 300 degrees. Gently remove the ham from the liquid and place in an ovenproof dish, covered with aluminum foil. Place in the oven and reduce the heat to 200 degrees until the ham is heated through.

STRAIN the solid ingredients from the liquid and discard them. Put the broth in a clean pot and simmer to reduce the liquid to a nice pan gravy of approximately 3 cups in volume. Set aside, keeping warm until you are ready to add it to the Wild Morels recipe below.

THIS dish is best served family style, presenting the entire roast on a cutting board and allowing the guest of honor the opportunity to carve it. Place the rice in a nice stone crock and the mushrooms in a separate serving bowl.

Serves 8

For the Red Wine Risotto

2 pounds Arborio or Carnaroli rice
½ cup onion, diced
1 ounce garlic, minced
2 tablespoons olive oil

1 bottle red table wine
6 cups chicken stock, heated
1 stick (4 ounces) butter, cut in cubes
2 cups grated Parmesan cheese

PLACE the olive oil in a large saucepan and gently sauté the rice, onion, and garlic over medium heat. Add the red wine and increase the heat to medium high, stirring constantly until almost all of the liquid is gone. Add about ⅓ of the chicken stock, stirring until most of the liquid is gone. Continue in this manner until all of the liquid has been incorporated and the rice is cooked. Remove from heat and fold in the butter chunks and then the Parmesan cheese.

For the Wild Morels

¼ pound bacon
2 tablespoons butter
2 pounds wild morel mushrooms
1 tablespoon garlic, minced

1 cup red wine
1 cup chicken stock
3 cups stock from the elk ham

IN A non-reactive skillet over medium low heat, render the fat from the bacon. Discard the bacon and add the butter. When the butter has melted, add the mushrooms and garlic, sautéing briefly. Add the wine and stock and cook until all the liquid is absorbed. Add the reduced stock from the elk ham and remove from heat. Keep warm until serving.

FLATHEAD CHERRY ICE CREAM

This ice cream is delicious by itself, but I also like to make large chocolate chip cookies and place a layer of ice cream in between two cookies to make an ice cream sandwich.

Ingredients

4 pounds Flathead cherries, pitted
3 cups sugar

1 lemon, juiced
½ gallon heavy cream, heated

Preparation

IN A heavy bottomed saucepan, cook the cherries, sugar, and lemon juice until a thick syrup forms. Lift out ⅓ of the cherries and reserve them. Puree the remaining fruit and syrup; fold into the hot cream and refrigerate until the mixture is cooled.

POUR the cooled mixture into an ice cream maker and follow the manufacturer's directions. You may need to do this in a couple of batches. While the ice cream is soft, fold in the reserved whole cherries.

ALLOW the ice cream to firm up overnight if you want it hard, or serve it immediately if you want softer ice cream.

Serves 8

Pollo Grill

Rotisserie & Bar

POLLO GRILL
ROTISSERIE & WINE BAR

Established 1998

1705 Wisconsin Avenue
Whitefish, MT 59937
406-863-9400
pollogr@bigsky.net
www.pollogrill.com

Reservations@pollogrill.com
Open 7 days, serving dinner
5:00 to 10:00 pm nightly

Pollo Grill

Walter and Susan Nickerson, Owners
Walter Nickerson, Chef

Walter and Susan Nickerson opened the Pollo Grill on April 1, 1998. Since that time the restaurant has enjoyed much critical acclaim and wide popularity with locals and visitors alike. The menus and wine lists are ever changing to keep abreast of seasonal and market availability. Recently the Pollo won the Wine Spectator Award of Excellence. The atmosphere at the Pollo Grill is comfortable and casual and the attentive service ensures a wonderful experience. The well-trained staff offers insight to all questions of preparation and is quick to offer wine-paring suggestions.

Off-premises catering is another facet to the Pollo Grill. Walter has developed a fine reputation for producing, preparing, and serving dinner parties, cocktail parties, weddings, and reunions. The Pollo Grill can supply everything from planning, rentals of all equipment, setup and breakdown, and of course, all food, beverage, and service staff.

Summer brings many special items to the Flathead Valley, so the Pollo Grill shares the local bounty by featuring fresh fruits, vegetables, and meats throughout the season. They have a wide variety of specials for the season, including Montana grown elk, trout, and a delectable rack of lamb.

Statewide, Montana is home to some of the world's greatest trophy-trout streams and lakes. This allows the Pollo Grill to feature local delicacies such as Rainbow Trout in a Tricolored Tortilla Crust with Cilantro Lime Sauce.

The legendary cherry orchards around Flathead Lake bloom in the spring and then produce lush, succulent white or bing cherries in early to mid-July. Walter teams these cherries with a specially seasoned Grilled Boneless Duck Breast, thinly sliced and generously sauced with these truly delicious native Montana cherries.

Both peppermint and wintergreen mint are grown here and used primarily for their very rich and strong oils. Some of this mint flavors a Mint Sauce which complements the Grilled Rack of Lamb.

Whitefish is regarded nationwide as an authentic recreation hot spot with boundless year-round activities and attractions because of its close proximity to Glacier National Park.

 Award of Excellence

STEAMED LITTLENECK CLAMS
with Chorizo, Fennel, Garlic, and White Wine

We recently have uncovered a great supply of littleneck clams available to us on a very regular basis. This recipe is an adaptation to a well-known Portuguese preparation and uses the Mexican chorizo in place of the chourice. The texture of the chorizo gives the resulting broth more body and just screams to be sopped up with some great crusty bread. It is a simple, quick, and delicious appetizer.

Ingredients

2 pounds littleneck clams (Manila or mahogany clams can be substituted)

8 ounces chorizo

½ fennel bulb, julienne

2 garlic cloves, finely diced

2 cups white wine (the crispness of Pinot Gris or Sauvignon Blanc works best)

2 tablespoons of olive oil

Preparation

HEAT the olive oil in a 4-quart saucepan.

ADD the chorizo and sauté, stirring often until some color occurs (4 minutes).

ADD garlic and fennel; sauté another 2 minutes. Add clams and wine. Cover and cook until all clams have opened. Discard any that don't open. Serve in shallow bowls with plenty of crusty bread.

OUR suggestions for accompanying wines would be the Duck Pond Pinot Gris or the Omak Sauvignon Blanc.

Serves 4

Osso Bucco
with Gorgonzola and Rosemary Risotto

At the Pollo Grill we have chosen "comfort food" as our focus. Although the Rotisserie is a real focal point in our kitchen, one can always find daily features that revolve around the hearty, simple and more often classic methods of cooking. This recipe for Osso Bucco fits all of these categories.

Ingredients for the Osso Bucco

4 2-inch thick veal foreshanks
1 cup flour
2 cloves of garlic, finely diced
1 28-ounce can of crushed tomatoes

2 cups white wine (the other half of the bottle from the steamed clam recipe)
Salt and pepper

Gremulata

Zest of one lemon
½ bunch of parsley, chopped finely

2 cloves of garlic, finely diced

Risotto

2 cups arborio rice
5 cups chicken stock or broth
1 cup crumbled Gorgonzola cheese

2 tablespoons finely chopped fresh rosemary
2 tablespoons of olive oil

Cooking Instructions for the Osso Bucco

PREHEAT oven to 350°F.

DREDGE the veal foreshanks in the flour and brown in olive oil in a braising pan. When you have seared all surfaces and see a light browning, add the garlic and continue to brown for an additional minute or two. Add the crushed tomatoes and white wine, season with salt and pepper. Cover and place the pan in a preheated 350°F oven. After 1 hour, turn the oven down to 250°F and continue to cook for a total of 3 hours. You can hold your Osso Bucco in a warm 200°F oven for some time. It will want to fall off the bone.

Cooking Instructions for the Risotto

RISOTTO does take some attention, 15–20 minutes.

HEAT the chicken stock in a saucepan. In another pan, heat the olive oil and add the arborio rice, stirring so as to coat the rice thoroughly with the oil. Start adding the hot chicken stock 2 or 3 ounces at a time. Let the stock be absorbed and continue adding the stock slowly until rice has become soft. You want to add the stock slowly so a cream-like liquid develops. When the rice is soft, add the Gorgonzola cheese and rosemary, stirring to blend completely.

Cooking Instructions for the Gremulata

THIS is the simple part. Just mix together the lemon zest, parsley, and garlic. Although this could be looked at as just a garnish, rarely will you find anything that sets off the flavors in any dish as this does for Osso Bucco.

Presentation

ON A large dinner plate, we like to serve the Risotto in the center of the plate with the veal shank off to the side slightly. Generously spoon on the braising sauce from the skillet in which the Osso Bucco was cooked and top with the Gremulata. For the purist, we would also serve with a marrow scoop.

Serves 4

Wine suggestions are wide open; any full-bodied Cabernet pairs wonderfully with this hearty dish and always any Borolo or Chianti Antinori Chianti Classico, Aldo Morenco Barbera Pirona, Carmenet Dynamite Cabernet Sauvignon.

CANNOLI WITH SHAVED CHOCOLATE

If you were inclined to serve this entire menu we think something on the light side would be a wonderful finale. Our Cannolis are just that, and to top that off even further we suggest a half bottle of Nivole Muscat d'asti.

Ingredients

8 prepared cannoli shells*
2 pound ricotta cheese
2 cups confectioners' sugar

1 teaspoon vanilla extract
1 teaspoon almond extract
1 block semi-sweet chocolate

Preparation

PLACE the ricotta in a fine mesh sieve and drain completely. Add the sugar and extracts and whip with a fine piano wire whip until smooth. Pipe the Ricotta mixture into the shells using a pastry bag and a medium star tip.

GRATE the chocolate directly over the cannolis so that they become sprinkled generously. Serve two to a person.

*Prepared cannoli shells can be purchased at specialty food stores or ordered off the Internet (see Culinary Sources, page 233).

Tupelo
Grille &
Wine Bar

Establised in 1995

17 Central Avenue
Whitefish, MT 59937
406–862–6136

Dinner served daily at 5:30 pm
(Reservations accepted only for
parties of six or more)

Tupelo Grille & Wine Bar

Missy & Patrick Carloss, Owners
Patrick Carloss, Chef

Patrick Carloss,

Southern cooking in Montana? No matter what the temperature is outside, Tupelo Grille on Central Avenue is always one of Whitefish's hottest dining spots. The Tupelo Grille was established in 1995 by Patrick and Missy Carloss, and it has quickly become one of Montana's favorites for locals and tourists alike. Specializing in Cajun Creole cuisine, Louisianan chef and owner Patrick Carloss provides a unique dining experience with a taste of the bayou.

Along with Carloss's terrific menu came a new sophistication in décor. Southern folk art and photography line the textured walls. Local diners, along with skiers from nearby Big Mountain, cluster in wooden booths and sneak peeks into the kitchen. Recently, the restaurant's wine list received a Wine Spectator Award.

While you're in Whitefish, look into the abundance of outdoor activities in the area—only 30 minutes from the West Glacier entrance to Glacier National Park, 30 minutes to Flathead Lake, and 10 minutes from Big Mountain Ski Resort. Whitefish's 1910 train depot still accommodates passengers daily as Amtrak passes through, making it an ideal train trip from the Northwest's major cities.

Y Award of Excellence

FENNEL-RUBBED PORK TENDERLOIN
with Orange Glaze and Roasted Yams

For the Pork

2 pounds pork tenderloin (silver skins removed)
4 tablespoons paprika
2 tablespoons ground fennel
2 tablespoons sugar
2 tablespoons salt
2 tablespoons garlic powder
1 tablespoon white pepper

PREHEAT oven to 375°F.

COMBINE all seasonings in shallow bowl. Place tenderloin into seasonings and rub until heavily coated. Heat heavy large nonstick skillet over high heat. Add pork and sear until brown all over, turning occasionally (about 5 minutes). Roast pork in oven until thermometer registers 160°F (about 30 minutes).

For the Yams

3 large yams or sweet potatoes (washed, peeled, and chopped in half-inch cubes)
1 tablespoon fresh ground ginger
1 tablespoon brown sugar
½ tablespoon allspice
2 tablespoons olive oil
1 tablespoon fresh thyme

PREHEAT oven to 350°F.

COMBINE all ingredients in mixing bowl and transfer to baking dish. Roast in oven for approximately 30 minutes or until yams are tender.

For the Orange Glaze

2 cups veal stock or canned beef broth
4 tablespoons orange marmalade
1 teaspoon balsamic vinegar

COMBINE veal stock and marmalade in saucepan and heat until reduced by half.

ADD balsamic vinegar.

SLICE pork and fan over roasted yams, and ladle sauce over the top.

Serves 4

FENNEL CRUSTED HALIBUT
with Peach Chutney and Roasted Red Pepper Couscous

This dish can be sautéed in a pan, but the flavor of the fennel seasoning really comes out when char grilled.

Ingredients

4 halibut steaks
2 tablespoons fennel seed
1 teaspoon salt
1 teaspoon white pepper

1 teaspoon granulated garlic
Roasted Red Pepper Couscous (recipe follows)
Peach Chutney (recipe follows)

Preparation

HEAT the oven to 350 degrees. Place the fennel seeds on a small baking sheet and roast the seeds in the oven until light brown. Grind the toasted seeds until fine. In a small bowl, combine the seeds with the salt, white pepper, and the granulated garlic.

LIGHTLY season the halibut on both sides with the spice mixture. Sear the halibut in a pan or on your char grill. Halibut cooks quickly, so don't over cook it. It should be done about the same time as the couscous.

TO SERVE, place a portion of the couscous at the center of each plate. Place the halibut on the couscous. Place a portion of the peach chutney on top of the halibut.

For the Red Pepper Couscous

¼ cup red bell pepper, finely diced
¼ cup onion, finely diced
¼ canned roasted red pepper, pureed

1¼ cup chicken stock
1 cup couscous

SAUTÉ the diced red bell pepper and the onion for about 1 minute. Add chicken stock and pureed roasted red pepper. Bring to a boil and then add the couscous. Stir, cover, and turn off heat. The couscous will be done in about 6 to 7 minutes.

For the Peach Chutney

¼ cup brown sugar
¼ cup granulated sugar
⅜ cup cider vinegar
1 teaspoon crushed red pepper
½ teaspoon salt
1 teaspoon mustard seed

1 teaspoon garlic, minced
¼ cup pickled ginger, chopped
¼ cup raisins
¼ cup water
2 cups fresh peaches, chopped

BRING the sugars and vinegar to a low boil and then add everything but the peaches. Simmer on low until the raisins bloom, or plump up. Add the peaches and simmer slightly until thickened. Chutney can be prepared the day before and served either at room temperature or slightly warmed.

Serves 4

Wine suggestion: Leeuwin "Artist Series" Riesling, Australia – a dry Riesling

CREAMY SHIITAKE AND PORTABELLA BISQUE

For the Bisque

1 large portabella mushroom, stems removed, sliced thinly	2 tablespoons sweet sherry
2 cups shiitake mushrooms, stems removed, sliced thin	12 cups chicken broth or stock
2 cups button mushrooms	3 cups heavy whipping cream
1 large onion	3 cups water
1 tablespoon minced garlic	½ tablespoon fresh thyme
5 tablespoons butter	½ teaspoon salt
	¼ teaspoon white pepper
	3 tablespoons flour

IN PROCESSOR, finely chop onion and button mushrooms and transfer to medium saucepan on high heat with garlic and 2 tablespoons of butter. Sauté until onions have clarified. Deglaze pan with sherry. Add remaining ingredients, except for flour and remainder of butter, bring to a simmer. In separate saucepan, melt 3 tablespoons of butter and combine with flour, slowly whisking it into bisque. Serve with chopped chives.

Serves 4

CHOCOLATE CHIP MELTAWAY PIE A LA MODE

Ingredients

1 cup semi-sweet chocolate chips	¼ pound (1 stick) unsalted butter, melted
½ cup walnuts, chopped	½ cup all purpose flour
2 large eggs, beaten	1 teaspoon vanilla extract
½ cup packed light brown sugar	1 frozen 9-inch pie shell
½ cup granulated sugar	French vanilla ice cream

Preparation

HEAT oven to 350 degrees. In a large bowl, mix together the chocolate chips, walnuts and the beaten eggs. Add the sugars, butter, and flour stirring to combine. Stir in the vanilla extract. Pour into the pie shell and bake in the 350-degree oven for about 25 to 30 minutes. Let cool before serving.

TO SERVE, cut into wedges and top with French vanilla ice cream.

Serves 8 to 10

Rainbow Falls, Missouri River. F. Jay Haynes, photographer, summer 1880.

Tupelo Grille, Whitefish

Snowgoose
Grille
at
St. Mary
Lodge

SUMMER ADDRESS
(April 16 - October 14)
The Resort at Glacier,
St. Mary Lodge
St. Mary, MT 59417

Breakfast 7 – 11 a.m.
Lunch 11:30 a.m. – 4 p.m.
Dining 5:30 – 10:00 pm

FOR MORE INFO
Call or email
406-732-4431
1-800-368-3689
stmary@glcpark.com
www.glcpark.com

The Snowgoose Grille has a spectacular backdrop.

Snowgoose Grille
at St. Mary Lodge in
Glacier National Park

Roscoe Black, Owner
Bryan Motola, Chef

St. Mary Lodge got its start in the mid- to late twenties after the proprietors, Hugh and Margaret Black, met in Glacier. The year 1926 found Hugh Black working in Michigan and looking for a change of scenery. He heard that Chief Ranger Nick Carter was possibly hiring, so he and a friend fixed up a Ford Model T and drove across the country from Caro, Michigan. Hugh became a seasonal ranger fighting forest fires and helping with early park development.

When the road to Logan Pass was partially finished in 1930, Hugh became the first road patrolman in Glacier Park. This job included keeping traffic speed down and keeping bears out of the government road camps. He was furnished with a Ford pickup and a shotgun loaded with birdshot.

Margaret James grew up in St. Paul, Minnesota, and came to Glacier in 1928 as the executive secretary for the Park Company, which was then owned by the Great Northern Railroad. This beautiful lady met the dashing and handsome ranger and a budding romance ensued. Hugh and Margaret were married in 1932 and started St. Mary Lodge and Resort. He got a lease on the current St. Mary Lodge property with $1,000 and a month's paycheck, and started construction right away. He and his crew built one-room cabins as fast as they could. Visitors would ask if they had any more cabins available and they would answer, "No, but we'll have one by tonight." They would rent the cabins at noon while the carpenters were still working on them. They built more every year until they had over forty of these one-room cabins with wood stoves and water pails. These same cabins now house the seasonal employees. While work was being done on the cabins, Margaret played a major role in the operation of their first restaurant, The Curly Bear Cafe. She also did all the bookwork for the rapidly growing operation.

When World War II hit, gas shortages all but stopped visitor traffic in the Park. During this time, Hugh supplemented the resort's income by running cattle and cutting ice from frozen lakes for the Great Northern Railroad which ran from Williston, North Dakota to Spokane, Washington. This ice was used on hot summer days to keep products cool prior to the advent of the refrigerated car. Margaret was kept very busy with the running of St. Mary, but somehow, found time to raise six children, as well.

The Blacks continued their hard work at St. Mary and were rewarded in 1952 by the completion of St. Mary Lodge, which housed 27 new rooms, the gift shop, and the new

St. Mary Cafe. The lodge was remodeled in 1975 when the lounge area was added to the front and an addition was put on the gift shop. In 1989, the restaurant was expanded and remodeled into what you see today. The name "Snowgoose Grille" was added at that time, coming from a restaurant that the Blacks ran the previous three years on Big Mountain in Whitefish.

The internationally famous Snowgoose Grille is rated one of Montana's top eating establishments and offers the best dining in the area. A remodel of the interior of the Snowgoose has just been completed, giving it a wonderfully comfortable atmosphere. Their reputation as one of the West's finest buffalo restaurants has garnered features in The New York Times, Travel and Leisure Magazine, Northwest Travel Magazine, and numerous other publications. They offer a wide variety of buffalo specialties, including prime rib, steaks, homemade sausage, appetizers, burgers, meatloaf, and unique specials throughout the summer. All meals are prepared with care and imagination using the freshest ingredients, herbs, and seasonings, combined with their own dash of Western flair. A basket of their famous hot sourdough scones and honey butter accompanies each dinner. Make sure to save room for a homemade dessert, because the Snowgoose's pastry chefs have been creating scrumptious huckleberry delights for decades along with a wide array of mouth-watering treats. They serve breakfast, lunch, and dinner from late May to October.

Although St. Mary Lodge "The Resort at Glacier" has seen many changes and improvements since 1932, one thing has remained constant: St. Mary Lodge is a family-run operation committed to providing guests a quality experience when visiting Glacier. The Black family,

along with hundreds of past employees who are a part of St. Mary history, have succeeded in creating facilities that have earned St. Mary Lodge the reputation as the place to stay or visit when in Glacier.

Combining the breathtaking panoramic views of Glacier and their famous Montana hospitality, the Snowgoose Grille is a Glacier Park tradition and truly a must stop on any trip to Montana.

STUFFED PORTABELLA MUSHROOM

Ingredients

2 large portabella mushrooms, approximately 5-inches across

4 ounces goat cheese, at room temperature

½ teaspoon garlic, crushed

1 tablespoon fresh herb (basil, oregano, or thyme)

salt and pepper to taste

1 cup all purpose flour

1 large egg

1 cup Panko breadcrumbs

1 cup balsamic vinegar

1 tablespoon white or brown sugar to taste

frying oil

8 ounces baby spinach leaves

1 roasted red pepper, julienned

Preparation

REMOVE stem and gills from the mushrooms. Place the mushrooms on a flat surface, cup side up, and use a teaspoon to gently remove all the dark brown from the inside.

IN A small bowl, mix the goat cheese, garlic, herb, salt, and pepper. Spread half the cheese in the cup of each mushroom. There should be at least ¼ inch in each. If the cheese mixture is at room temperature, it will be easier to spread. Cut each mushroom in half.

SET UP a breading station with 3 containers. In the first container, combine the flour with salt and pepper. In the second, whip the egg and add a splash of water. Put the Panko breadcrumbs in the third container. Lightly dampen the outside of the mushroom, coat each half first with the flour, then egg, and finally a light layer of breadcrumbs. The mushrooms can be held in the refrigerator until they are ready to be cooked.

IN A small saucepan, simmer the balsamic vinegar over medium-low heat until reduced by half. Depending on the quality of the vinegar, you may need to add a tablespoon of sugar. Taste it first and decide if it should be sweeter. The reduction will become thicker as it cools.

USING a deep fryer or heavy skillet with at least 1 inch of oil set at 350 degrees, gently cook the mushrooms on both sides until golden in color; about 2 to 3 minutes per side. Remove from oil and place on a paper towel to drain.

TO SERVE, place a bed of spinach on each plate with just enough to cover the plate. Place a warm mushroom half on top of the spinach. Use a heaping tablespoon of the julienned roasted red pepper as a garnish on each mushroom. Finish by drizzling the balsamic reduction over the top of the finished dish.

Serves 4

BEER CHEESE SOUP

Ingredients

1⅞ ounces butter
1⅛ ounces onion, minced
1⅞ ounces flour
1½ cups turkey stock
1½ cups milk, 2% lowfat
⅜ cup heavy cream

1⅞ ounces Cheddar cheese, grated
1⅞ ounces American cheese, grated
¾ cup beer
1⅛ dashes cayenne pepper
1⅛ dashes celery salt

Preparation

IN A 2-quart saucepan melt butter over medium heat. Add onions, cook till soft. Do not burn. Add flour to make roux, let cook for 7-8 minutes. Keep stirring. Heat milk, cream, and stock in separate pan until it reaches 160°F. Whisk milk mixture and stock into roux. Add cheeses and mix until well blended and mix thickens. Add beer and seasonings. Let simmer for 5 minutes. (Do not let boil.) Salt and pepper to taste.

Serves 6

Lake McDonald in Glacier National Park.

SEARED DUCK SALAD

Ingredients

4　4 to 6 ounce boneless skin-on duck
　　breasts
　　balsamic vinegar
1　teaspoon salt
1　teaspoon pepper
4–8　wonton wrappers, depending on size

　　frying oil
4　cups, any combination of mixed baby
　　greens, arugula or baby spinach
1　cup blue cheese, crumbled
½　cup Candied Walnuts (recipe follows)
　　Balsamic Vinaigrette (recipe follows)

Preparation

MARINATE the duck breast in some balsamic vinegar for about 20 minutes. Don't waste the vinegar. A small layer in a flat dish that covers the breasts about halfway is enough. Turn breast and continue marinating another 20 minutes.

HEAT the oven to 350 degrees. Remove the duck breasts from the marinade and, using a sharp knife, score 4 ¼-inch deep cuts across the skin at a 45-degree angle. Sprinkle ¼ teaspoon salt and ¼ teaspoon pepper over the meat side of each duck breast.

HEAT a well-seasoned skillet or nonstick pan over high heat. When pan is hot, add duck breasts, skin side down, and cook for 5 minutes, or until skin is brown and crispy. Flip and cook for 2 more minutes. If you are unfamiliar with duck breasts, don't be put off by their unusual look. The fat-to-meat proportions reverse themselves when cooked, as much of the fat is rendered and the meat expands.

REMOVE pan from heat and transfer duck breasts, skin side up, to a cooking sheet lined with aluminum foil. Bake on the top rack of the 350-degree oven for 6 minutes.

CUT 4 to 8 wonton wrappers (depending on size) into ¼-inch strips. Separate all the layers. Using a deep fryer or a heavy skillet with at least 1 inch of oil set at 350 degrees, fry the strips until crisp. Remove from oil and place on a paper towel to drain.

TO SERVE, evenly divide the greens on 4 plates and top with the blue cheese and walnuts. Remove duck from the oven and slice each breast at a 45-degree angle into ¼-inch strips. If properly cooked, the duck should resemble medium-rare steak. Arrange the duck in a fanlike pattern on the top of the salad. Drizzle with the Balsamic Vinaigrette. Garnish with the fried wonton strips.

Serves 4

For the Candied Walnuts

1 pound shelled walnut halves (or pecans)
⅔ cup powdered sugar
1 teaspoon salt

2 pinches (approx. ¼ teaspoon) cayenne pepper or chili powder (optional)

HEAT the oven to 350 degrees. In a large bowl, mix the sugar, salt and cayenne. Set aside. Dip walnuts into boiling water just long enough to get them hot, approximately 20 to 30 seconds. Remove and shake off excess water. Dump the nuts in the bowl and mix well. Shake off any excess sugar, if there is any. Place the nuts in a single layer on an oiled sheet pan. Bake at 350 degrees for approximately 30 minutes, watching carefully. Do not let them burn.

Yield 1 pound

For the Balsamic Vinaigrette

¼ cup balsamic vinegar
1 tablespoon garlic, chopped
½ teaspoon salt
½ teaspoon freshly ground pepper

¾ cup olive oil
2 teaspoons dark brown sugar (optional)

BEAT the vinegar in a bowl with the garlic, salt and pepper until the salt dissolves. If using a good quality balsamic vinegar, you should not need the sugar, but if using a lesser quality you might want to add the sugar to round out the dressing. If you add the sugar, beat the mixture again until the sugar dissolves. Then beat in the oil by droplets, whisking constantly. You can also place the ingredients in a screw-top jar and shake to combine. Taste and adjust the seasonings.

Yield 1 cup

Strawberry Chicken Salad

For the Salad

6	grilled chicken breast halves, julienne	2	heads romaine lettuce, chopped
18	whole strawberries, sliced	1	batch Citrus Poppy Seed Dressing
3	slices red onion rounds		

TOSS romaine and strawberries with Citrus Poppy Seed Dressing. Divide equally among chilled salad plates. Top with a julienne chicken breast. Garnish with red onion rounds.

Serves 6

Citrus Poppy Seed Dressing

For the Dressing

2	cup sugar	3	cup lemon juice
1½	teaspoons salt	1	cup mayonnaise
1	teaspoon dry mustard	1½	tablespoons poppy seeds
1	tablespoon onion juice		

MIX sugar, salt, dry mustard, onion, and lemon juice and poppy seeds into the mayonnaise.

Serves (roughly) 8 salads

BUFFALO FLANK STEAK

For the Marinade

 1   pint beer (your favorite)
1⅓ cups Italian salad dressing
 ⅔ cup red wine
 ⅓ cup red wine vinegar
 ½ cup soy sauce
2⅔ tablespoons Worcestershire sauce
1⅓ tablespoons sesame oil

2⅔ tablespoons shallot, chopped
2⅔ tablespoons garlic, chopped
2⅔ tablespoons tomato paste
2⅔ tablespoons lime juice
 1   teaspoon coriander
 1   teaspoon white pepper
 1   teaspoon salt

For the Buffalo

 3   pounds buffalo flank steak

PREPARE a marinade of all ingredients and marinate steak a minimum of 6 hours, overnight is best.

BROIL steak over hot charcoal fire for 5 to 10 minutes on each side, depending on degree of rareness desired.

SLICE thinly across the grain and serve with Béarnaise sauce.

Serves 6

BÉARNAISE SAUCE

For the Sauce

 ½ cup white wine vinegar*
 3   each shallots, minced fine
 2   tablespoons fresh tarragon, minced

 ½ teaspoon white pepper
 2   sticks butter (1 cup)

PUT vinegar, shallots, half the tarragon, and pepper in a small saucepan. Bring to a boil and reduce until liquid is nearly gone. Cook at an extremely low heat and whisk in cubes of cold butter until it is all incorporated. (Do not let this boil.) If too thick, then whisk in a little hot water. Stir in remaining tarragon.

*You may use ¼ cup of white wine and 1/4 cup of white wine vinegar for a slightly different taste.

Huckleberry Mud Pie

Ingredients

1 pound Oreo cookies, filling removed
and cookies crushed

2 ounces sugar – liquid measure

3½ tablespoons butter, softened

1 gallon huckleberry ice cream, slightly
softened

3 cups hot fudge topping, warmed, not
hot

Preparation

HEAT oven to 325 degrees. In a bowl, combine the crushed Oreo with the sugar and butter. Mix well. Form the crust into a 9-inch springform pan. Bake the crust in the 325-degree oven for 15 minutes. Remove from oven and cool.

WHEN the crust is cool, start layering the ice cream and hot fudge topping, freezing each layer so that the ice cream will not melt when the fudge layer is added. It is important to freeze each layer as firmly as possible. Work quickly and return the pan to the freezer. Start with a layer of ice cream, approximately 5 cups. Then add a second layer of approximately 1 cup of fudge topping. Make sure the fudge is warm and not hot so that it doesn't melt the ice cream. Another trick is to add some water to the fudge to make it easier to spread. Add a third layer of ice cream, a fourth layer of fudge, a fifth layer of ice cream, and a final layer of fudge, making sure each layer freezes properly.

TO SERVE, allow the pie to temper for a few minutes so it can be cut easily. Remove the springform and cut in wedges. If huckleberry ice cream is not available, any berry or cherry ice cream will work.

Serves 12 to 16

Ristorante Portofino

220 Central Avenue
Great Falls, MT 59401
406-453-7186
Reservations recommended

Monday–Friday
11:00 am to 9:00 pm
Saturday 4:00 to 9:00 pm
Closed Sundays

The Ristorante Portofino

Tina Germano and Massimo Viale, Owners
Mike Taylor, Chef

Ristorante Portofino opened in the Christmas season of 1999. The restaurant is co-owned by mother and son, Tina Germano and Massimo Viale. Both are natives of Portofino, Italy. Portofino is a small port town just outside of Genoa filled with all types of ships and people.

Ristorante Portofino brings the feeling and the flavors from this spot on the northwest coast of Italy to Great Falls, Montana. This restaurant prides itself on an extensive menu of genuine Italian foods prepared from scratch in their kitchen and offers wonderful wines and coffees made in authentic Italian style.

They are located in the heart of Great Falls, just steps away from the Civic Center, Paris-Gibson Square, and many interesting shops, art galleries, antique shops, and downtown hotels. It is their pleasure to bring a little of Italy into to your life while visitng Great Falls.

Make sure to visit the new Lewis and Clark Interpretive Center on the outskirts of Great Falls. Cultural exhibits and outdoor trails detail the 1804-1806 journey of the Lewis and Clark Expedition with focus on their interactions with the Plains Indians.

Our artist (F. Gary Haynes) at the Great Falls of the Missouri. (Summer 1880)

Asparagus Rollatine

This makes a wonderful appetizer or can be served as a meal with an accompanying side dish.

Ingredients

2 fresh tomatoes (Roma or regular)
½ cup onion, chopped
2 teaspoons basil
2 teaspoons parsley
4 teaspoons chopped garlic
1-2 teaspoons olive oil
   Salt and pepper to taste

8 asparagus spears
2 slices of provolone cheese
2 slices of prosciutto
   Flour
3-4 eggs
   Bread crumbs

Preparation

IN A medium-sized bowl, dice the tomatoes and half of the onion. Chop about 2 teaspoons of basil and parsley. Also chop about 4 teaspoons of garlic. Add 1-2 teaspoons of olive oil and salt and pepper to taste. Mix gently to combine and add basil, parsley, garlic, or pepper and salt as needed. Heat a medium-sized pan of water and blanch the asparagus spears. Wrap four of the spears with a slice of provolone and one slice of prosciutto. Then pass the wrap through flour, eggs, and finally, bread crumbs. Repeat for the other four spears. Then fry the wrapped asparagus and serve topped with the tomato mixture.

Serves 2

CHICKEN VALDOSTANA

This dish is a long-standing favorite on our dinner menu. A true Italian specialty, it is sure to make your mouth water.

Ingredients

1 whole boneless, skinless chicken breast
Thinly-sliced prosciutto
Mozzarella cheese
Fresh spinach
3-4 eggs, beaten

Bread crumbs
Flour
Garlic
Olive oil (extra virgin preferably)
Salt and pepper

For the Sauce

Brown gravy
Marsala wine

Mushrooms
Artichoke hearts

BEFORE cooking, pour the flour into one medium-sized bowl, and do likewise with the bread crumbs and eggs. Each should be in a separate bowl. Also mince or mash the garlic into a pan with about ⅓ cup of olive oil.

Preparation

SPLIT the chicken breast into two even halves. Remove any excess fat. Then slice the two halves horizontally into four pieces and pound out the four pieces.

For the Stuffing

SAUTÉ 8 ounces of spinach and garlic and olive oil; salt and pepper to taste. Then place 1 piece of prosciutto, a slice of mozzarella, and 4 ounces of the spinach between 2 halves of the chicken breast. Repeat this for the other halves of the breast. Then, to ensure that the stuffing stays in, pound the outer edges of the breast together. Take the stuffed breast and pass it through the flour, eggs, and then the bread crumbs. Then fry the chicken.

PREHEAT oven to 400°F.

IN A separate pan, add 1 cup of brown gravy, 2 ounces of Marsala wine. Toss in a handful of mushrooms and two artichoke hearts. Once the chicken is thoroughly fried, add it to the saucepan and place in the oven on high heat for approximately 15 minutes. Serve the chicken on a dish with veggie of choice or potatoes.

Serves 2

The
Union
Grille

Established in 1882

1 Grand Union Square
Fort Benton, MT 59442
406-662-1882 or 1-888-838-1882
grandunion@3rivers.net
www.grandunionhotel.com
Reservations recommended

Summer Dining: Tuesday – Sunday
5:00 p.m. – 9:00 p.m.
Winter Dining: Wednesday – Saturday
5:00 p.m. – 9:00 p.m.
Sunday 4:00 p.m. – 8:00 p.m.

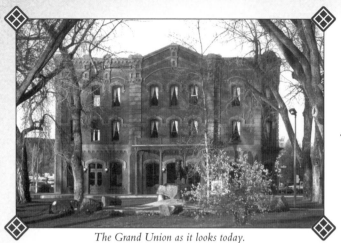
The Grand Union as it looks today.

The Grand Union
Montana's Oldest Operating Hotel

James & Cheryl Gagnon, Owners

The Grand Union Hotel gained a new lease on life following an award-winning restoration, supervised by the National Trust for Historic Preservation, the U.S. Parks Department, and the Montana State Historic Preservation Office, that preserved the historical character of Montana's oldest operating hotel and one of its most famous landmarks.

The hotel's history began in 1882, just 36 years after Fort Benton was founded and 7 years before Montana became a state. It was built at the height of Fort Benton's prosperity during the steamboat era on the Upper Missouri River.

With construction costs of $50,000, and with an additional $150,000 spent on furnishings, the newly christened Grand Union Hotel opened November 2, 1882 with the biggest party the city and territory had ever seen.

Within a year, however, the hotel's fortunes declined. The opening of the Northern Pacific Railroad to Helena in June and the Canadian Pacific Railroad to Calgary in 1883 dealt a mortal blow to Fort Benton and the Grand Union Hotel with the closing of the territory's most important highway, the Missouri River. Business in Fort Benton declined rapidly and in early 1884 the hotel failed and was sold at a sheriff's sale in May of that year.

Operating through Fort Benton's decline and the ascendance of newly established Great Falls nearby, the hotel continued to suffer and was sold to Mr. J. H. Green and Mr. B. F. O'Neal in 1899 for just $10,000. Messrs. Green and O'Neal undertook a major renovation of the hotel, installing steam heat, electricity, and men and women's toilets on every floor. Elaborate furnishings were sold or discarded and new fashionable oak and brass furnishings were installed together with a quarter-sawn oak faux paint finish over the varnished woodwork. Enamel found its way onto the upstairs woodwork at this time and the black walnut bar received a coat of white paint.

In 1917, with the world at war and the Homestead land boom on in Montana, local ranchers, Mr. and Mrs. Charles Lepley bought the Grand Union. In just two years, Prohibition closed the hotel's thriving saloon and dry weather, poor crops and falling prices brought on the Great Depression to Montana.

During the 1930s and '40s the Grand Union ran steadily downhill due to the dire economic conditions of the area. The bedrooms, once considered the "best in the West," gained

a reputation for a permanent insect population and worn and broken furnishings.

In the mid-1940s the Depression ended as agriculture rose to undisputed importance in Fort Benton and Chouteau County. In 1952, the hotel was sold again, this time to Mr. and Mrs. Harold Thomas. By then, the lobby, dining room, and saloon were ghosts of a once elegant era. Rooms were threadbare with straw mattresses still sprawling on sagging springs. Two public bathrooms on each of the three floors were the only personal sanitary facilities in the hotel. Upstairs, pieces of the once picturesque chimneys sometimes fell to the sidewalk due to weathering. Bats nested in cavities in the cornices. Soot from the chimneys sifted down the walls and birds flew in and out at will. The window frames were so loose in their masonry that a person could stick his hand through the cracks. Sun had warped the window moldings badly. Settlement of the building made the upper floors sag.

Mr. Thomas completed a one-man, multi-year restoration that is credited with saving the building. By the late '70s, Mr. and Mrs. Thomas were interested in retiring, but wanted to see the hotel pass into responsible hands interested in its preservation. Rejecting various offers interested only in salvaging the hotel's contents, antiques and brickworks, they agreed to sell the hotel in 1979 to a group of local farmers headed by Mr. and Mrs. Roger DeBruycker.

In 1983, the hotel was closed for renovation. Prior to completion, however, the project collapsed due to a failed financing plan and inadequate capitalization. In 1986, the hotel was sold at sheriff's sale to satisfy debts, and the building's contents were stripped and sold at public auction by the DeBruyckers. The building was then left abandoned pending sale until 1995 when native Montanans James and Cheryl Gagnon purchased it with a plan to restore and reopen the century-old hotel.

An elegantly restored room.

The Grand Union Hotel was elegantly restored to its original splendor, re-opening on its 117th anniversary on November 2, 1999. Today, listed on the National Register of Historic Places, and recipient of various state and national restoration awards, the Grand Union Hotel is Montana's oldest operating hotel and proud to continue its tradition by once again providing one of the grandest lodging and dining experiences in Montana.

The Union Grille, Fort Benton

215

WILD SALMON

with Tomato Basil Vinaigrette and Sweet Onion Salad

If wild salmon is not available, you can use any other dark-fleshed fish. Serve this dish with your favorite roasted potato recipe for a complete meal in one dish.

Ingredients

4 8-ounce wild salmon
salt and pepper to taste

Tomato and Basil Vinaigrette (recipe follows)
Sweet Onion Salad (recipe follows)

Preparation

SEASON salmon with salt and pepper and broil over your barbeque or oven roast in a 450-degree oven until medium.

TO SERVE, place roasted potatoes in individual pasta bowls. Place salmon on top of potatoes and drizzle Tomato and Basil Vinaigrette over entire plate. Top with Sweet Onion Salad.

Serves 4

For the Tomato and Basil Vinaigrette

10 Roma tomatoes
2 ounces fresh basil
2 ounces rice vinegar

¾ cup canola oil
¼ cup olive oil
salt and pepper to taste

IN A blender, puree tomatoes with basil. Add rice vinegar and blend until smooth. Slowly add in canola and olive oils. Adjust seasoning by adding salt and pepper to taste. You can strain this vinaigrette through a fine mesh strainer, if you wish.

For the Sweet Onion Salad

1 sweet onion, Walla Walla or Vidalia, julienned
1 cup cherry tomatoes, quartered
1 tablespoon salt

1 teaspoon pepper
fresh parsley, chopped (optional)
fresh basil, chopped (optional)

PLACE julienned sweet onion in a bowl, add salt and pepper and let stand for 10 minutes. Add tomatoes and toss to combine. Add parsley and basil, if you wish, and toss to combine. Keep cool until ready to serve.

Union Rubbed Rib Steak

Ingredients

4 16-ounce rib steaks
1 tablespoon salt
1 tablespoon garlic powder
1 tablespoon paprika
1 tablespoon lemon pepper

1 tablespoon chili powder
1 tablespoon ground cumin
4 tablespoons sugar
2 teaspoons black pepper

Preparation

MIX all the dry ingredients together to make a seasoned salt. Generously rub on both sides of steaks. Let stand 10 minutes at room temperature. Grill until desired temperature is achieved, about 4 minutes per side for medium rare.

SERVE with your favorite mashed potatoes or roasted root vegetables.

Serves 4

Fort Benton, Montana T.C. Power Store. (ca. 1870's)

The River Grille

1225 Custer Avenue
Helena, MT 59601
406-442-1075
www.rivergrille.com

Hours of Operation
Tuesday-Saturday
5 pm to 10 pm
Open year-round

The River Grille

Laura Fix and Ron Morris,
General Managers
Ron Morris, Chef

The River Grille is owned and operated by the Morris family of Helena, who has served restaurant patrons in the Helena area for over 75 years.

The River Grille opened in January of 1997 to great reviews. Co-owners Ron Morris and his wife Laura Fix operate the restaurant for the family. Laura, a baker by trade, runs the front-of-the-house operations and Ron, a Certified Executive Chef with the American Culinary Federation, runs the kitchen.

It is an upscale Euro Montana Bistro with casual dining in an elegant atmosphere. Great Montana steaks and prime rib are featured, with fresh seafood and unique specials being offered daily. The River Grille serves one of the largest Single Malt Scotch collections in Montana!

The River Grille is located in Helena—the City of Gold, the Queen City of the Rockies. The city was originally a mining camp that sprang up when gold, silver, and copper were discovered in the valley. Helena became the territorial capital and once had more millionaires than any other city in the United States.

Today Helena is the home of the Montana state capitol and a variety of businesses. Southwestern Montana's revitalized mining and metals processing industries are located here, and it is still rich in agricultural tradition.

The River Grille, Helena

CREAM OF FOUR-ONION SOUP
This is the Signature Soup at the River Grille

Ingredients

1 stick butter (¼ pound)
1 pound onions, sliced ¼-inch thick)
1 clove garlic, minced
6 ounces leeks (white and green tender
   parts), sliced ¼-inch thick
2 ounces shallots, minced
½ ounce fresh ginger, minced
   Pinch of cayenne pepper
4 ounces flour
2 quarts chicken stock or broth

1¼ cups dry white wine
4¼ cups whipping cream
2 tablespoons brandy
1 tablespoon plus 1 teaspoon fresh
   lemon juice
1 tablespoon kosher salt
2 teaspoons white pepper
2 teaspoons sugar
   Durkee's Fried Onions, for garnish
   fresh chives, minced, for garnish

Preparation

HEAT butter in heavy-gauged soup pot over low heat. Add onions and sauté lightly for 10 minutes. Add sugar and simmer 10 minutes more. Add leeks, shallots, ginger, garlic, and cayenne. Cook 3-5 minutes, stirring frequently; add flour and let cook for 3-5 more minutes. Slowly mix in chicken stock and wine. Bring soup to a boil. Reduce to a simmer and add cream. Let soup reduce for 30 minutes. Add brandy, lemon juice, salt and pepper; let simmer for 15 minutes longer. Cool soup quickly in an ice-water bath and refrigerate overnight. Soup improves in flavor as it sits.

TO SERVE, heat soup in double boiler to 140-150°F. Garnish with fried onions and fresh chives.

Serves 8

TAGLIATELLE BOLOGNESE, LASAGNA STYLE

Ingredients

1   pound lean ground beef
1   pound hot Italian sausage
4   tablespoons garlic, minced & divided
½   teaspoon red chile peppers, dried and chopped
3   pounds pear tomatoes, diced
3   large red peppers, roasted and cut into ½-inch strips
1   cup fresh parsley, minced

1   tablespoon oregano
4   teaspoons salt, divided
1   teaspoon pepper, course grind
½   cup olive oil
¼   pound butter
1   quart whipping cream
1   teaspoon pepper
1   pound lasagna noodles, cooked
3   cups Parmesan cheese, shredded

Preparation

HEAT a large braising pan over medium-high heat. When pan is hot, add sausage and ground beef, a little at a time so that temperature doesn't drop rapidly. Meat should sizzle and smoke. Let meat brown on one side, and then stir. Meat should be cooked to medium rare. Drain off excess fat. Add 2 tablespoons of the minced garlic, the chile pepper, tomatoes, red peppers, parsley, oregano, 2 teaspoons of the salt, and the course grind pepper. Simmer, uncovered, about 30 minutes until flavors blend and sauce thickens. Stir in olive oil to bind sauce. Set aside, and let sauce cool.

IN A medium saucepan, melt butter over medium-high heat. Add the rest of the garlic and simmer 2–3 minutes. Add whipping cream, the remaining 2 teaspoons salt and 1 teaspoon pepper. Simmer on low heat until sauce is reduced by one-third. Remove from heat and let cool while cooking the lasagna noodles.

HEAT oven to 350 degrees. To assemble the Tagliatelle, combine the cream sauce and meat sauce in a large container. Begin layering the ingredients in a large casserole or rectangular cake pan. Start with a layer of the meat and cream sauce, followed by cooked noodles, and then a layer of shredded Parmesan cheese. Use all the ingredients and end with a layer of sauce.

COVER pan with foil and bake in 350-degree oven for 1 hour. Remove from oven and let rest at room temperature for 30 minutes to set.

Serves 6

Two-Course Pizza Dinner for Two

One Half of Pizza—Prosciutto & Artichoke with Four Wisconsin Cheeses
Other Half of Pizza—Wisconsin Brie with Apples and Toasted Pine Nuts

Ingredients

- 1 12-inch pizza crust
- 6 ounces pizza sauce
- 2 ounces Parma prosciutto, sliced 8 x 8 x 1 inch
- 2 ounces artichoke hearts, cut in 8-inch pieces
- 4 ounces of 4 cheese blends, grated (equal parts Wisconsin Cheddar, Wisconsin Muenster, Wisconsin Parmesan, Wisconsin Provolone)

- ½ cup apricot preserves
- 5 ounces Wisconsin Brie–sliced ⅛ inch
- 1 large Granny Smith apple-cored, ⅛-inch slices, halved
- 1 tablespoon toasted pine nuts
- 2 tablespoon cinnamon sugar

Preparation

HEAT oven to 375° (convection) or 425° (conventional).

SPREAD pizza sauce over half of crust; spread apricot preserves over the other half of crust.

ARRANGE prosciutto over the pizza sauce and top with the four cheese blend. Arrange the artichokes neatly on top of the cheese. (This is a two-sided pizza. Be careful during assembly to keep the appropriate ingredients on the appropriate half of the crust.) Lay the slices of brie over the apricot side of the crust and arrange the apples neatly over the brie.

SPRINKLE the pine nuts over the brie and apples. Sift the cinnamon sugar over the top of the apple/brie side.

BAKE in preheated oven for 10 minutes (conventional oven) or 10-12 minutes (convection oven).

ALLOW pizza to rest for 3-5 minutes before slicing.

Serves 2

Steamers 'Benton' and 'Helena', Poplar Creek.
(Summer 1880)

Steamer 'Helena' cabin (interior).
(Summer 1880)

Fly Fishers Inn

2629 Old U.S. Hwy. 91
Cascade, MT 59421
406-468-2529
fish@flyfishersinn.com
www.flyfishersinn.com

Open to fly-fishing guests daily
Open to the public, Friday and
Saturday at 7:00 pm
Call for Reservations and
Information

The Fly Fishers Inn

Rick and Lynne Pasquale, Owners
Lynne Pasquale, Chef

The Fly Fishers Inn is nestled in a scenic canyon on the Missouri River.

Little did Lewis and Clark realize that the path of their trek in 1805 would eventually be viewed from a fly-fishing lodge complete with gourmet dining. Nestled in the Missouri Canyon, Fly Fishers Inn offers you comfort and convenience in a country setting. Overlooking the river at the foot of Mountain Palace Rock, the lodge houses the kitchen and dining room. The guest rooms are in a separate building, which was built in 1991 when the Pasquales purchased the property.

The original concept was to have a fly-fishing lodge serving unique meals to accommodate their fishing clients. It was an opportunity for Chef Lynne and Angler Rick to work together again.

The quality of the fishing on the Missouri River led the Pasquales to move from the East to Montana in 1981. It was never their intention to have the Inn. They started an outfitting business in 1985 operating out of Great Falls. The number of clients fishing the Missouri increased each year, until they saw a need for a location to lodge and feed their clients—and what better place than on the Missouri in the heart of fantastic fishing.

After a number of executive retreats were held at the Inn, Great Falls and Helena residents soon discovered the culinary ability of Lynne Pasquale. The Pasquales agreed to open the Inn for dinner to local gourmets on a reservation basis from April to December.

The pris-fixe, five course menus are published about every six weeks for the Friday and Saturday seating. With the current emphasis on healthy eating, the challenge has been to keep uniqueness, taste, and flavor while reducing the unhealthy ingredients. But don't look for this in Lynne's desserts.

The building that houses the lodge was originally built in 1936 when the "new" road between Helena and Great Falls was funded as part of the Depression economic recovery program. The business was a typical Montana roadside restaurant/bar that catered to those traveling between cities. It also served as an after church meeting place where families met and a spot where fishermen would stop to have something to eat or drink. When the Interstate was built in the late 1960s the building was bypassed and business declined.

Things have changed a lot since then. Lynne Pasquale's recipes and culinary skills have been published in a number of national magazines, including *Sunset* and *Town and Country*, as well as in her new cookbook, *"Recipes from the Fly Fisher's Inn."*

GARLIC SOUP

Ingredients

3 tablespoons unsalted butter
1 large yellow onion, chopped –
approximately 21 ounces
6 medium Idaho potatoes, peeled &
chopped – approximately 30 ounces
1 whole head garlic, minced –
approximately 15 cloves

5 cups chicken stock or broth
1 teaspoon salt
½ teaspoon pepper to taste
½ cup heavy cream or whipping cream
Garlic-Parsley Butter (recipe follows)

Preparation

MELT butter in a Dutch oven over medium heat. Add onion and sauté until the onion is translucent, about 5 minutes. Add potatoes, stock, garlic, salt, and pepper. Heat to boiling. Reduce heat and simmer uncovered until potatoes are tender, about 20 minutes. Process the soup in batches in a blender or food processor fitted with a steel blade. Strain through a sieve back into the Dutch oven and reheat over low heat. Stir in cream and adjust seasonings to taste.

TO SERVE, ladle into soup bowls and top each serving with a slice of Garlic-Parsley butter.

Serves 9

For the Garlic–Parsley Butter

¼ cup fresh parsley leaves
2 garlic cloves, minced

4 tablespoons butter, softened

PROCESS butter and parsley in a food processor fitted with a steel blade, until parsley is finely chopped. Add minced garlic and process just to combine. Spread butter mixture on waxed paper and shape into a log. Freeze until ready to serve. Cut the garlic-parsley butter into thin slices when ready to serve.

Vegetable Couscous

While the dressing makes this a delicious entrée on its own, you can also serve it without the dressing if it is accompanying an entrée that already has a sauce.

Ingredients

2½ cups chicken broth
1¾ cups couscous
2 carrots, shredded
2 cups tomato, seeded & finely diced
½ cup red bell pepper, diced
½ cup green bell pepper, diced
½ cup celery, diced
½ teaspoon grated lemon rind

¼ cup green onions, thinly sliced
¼ cup fresh parsley, chopped
3 tablespoons balsamic vinegar
1 tablespoon olive oil
1 tablespoon Dijon mustard
¼ teaspoon black pepper
salt to taste

Preparation

IN A medium saucepan, bring chicken broth to a boil and stir in couscous. Remove from heat and let stand, covered, for 5 minutes. Fluff with a fork. Uncover, and let cool.

IN A large bowl, combine couscous, carrot, tomato, bell peppers, celery, lemon rind, green onions, and parsley and toss gently. Combine vinegar, oil, mustard, and pepper in a small bowl, stirring with a wire whisk to emulsify. Add to couscous mixture, tossing to coat. Adjust seasoning with salt to taste. Serve at room temperature or chilled.

Serves 10 as a side dish

SWORDFISH, HALIBUT, OR MAHI
with Roasted Red Pepper Basil Mayonnaise

Ingredients

4 8-ounce fish fillets
1 cup bottled roasted red peppers, drained
6 tablespoons low-fat mayonnaise
2 tablespoons Dijon mustard

2 garlic cloves, minced
½ teaspoon lemon juice
   salt and pepper to taste
1 cup fresh basil leaves, washed well and spun dry

Preparation

IN A blender or food processor, puree red peppers, mayonnaise, mustard, garlic, lemon juice, and salt and pepper to taste. Transfer 2 tablespoons of mayonnaise mixture to a small bowl and reserve. Place the rest of mayonnaise in another bowl. Chop the basil leaves by hand, so they won't blacken. Mix the chopped basil into the mayonnaise mixture and keep cool until ready to serve.

RINSE and pat the fish filets dry. Spread the reserved 2 tablespoons of mayonnaise mixture on 1 side of each filet. Grill, broil, or bake fish to desired doneness and serve with red pepper basil mayonnaise. If you wish to bake the filets: swordfish will take about 11 minutes in a 450-degree oven, and halibut or mahi will take 10 to 12 minutes in a 350-degree oven.

Serves 4

Veal with Balsamic Vinegar and Sage

Ingredients

4   5-ounce portions veal scaloppini
2   tablespoons flour
½   teaspoon salt
⅛   teaspoon freshly ground pepper
1   tablespoon unsalted butter

1   tablespoon olive or vegetable oil
⅔   cup balsamic vinegar
¼   cup chicken stock or broth
1   tablespoon fresh sage, chopped – or 1
    teaspoon dried

Preparation

COMBINE flour, salt, and pepper. Dredge scaloppini in seasoned flour and shake off excess. In a large non-reactive skillet, melt the butter in the oil over moderately high heat. Working in 2 batches, add the scaloppini and cook until nicely browned, about 1½ minutes per side. Do not overcook. Transfer to a plate, cover with foil, and keep warm.

DRAIN the fat, if any, from the pan and add the vinegar. Boil, scraping the bottom of the pan with a wooden spoon to release any brown bits, until the mixture is thickened and reduced by about half. Add the chicken stock and any juices that have accumulated on the plate from the veal, and boil until reduced to a dark, shiny sauce, about 1 minute. Add the sage and season to taste with salt and pepper.

TO SERVE, arrange the scaloppini on a plate and spoon the sauce on top.

Serves 4

CAPPUCCINO-CHOCOLATE MOUSSE

This recipe can be doubled. Melt the chocolate in the espresso first, and then do the egg mixture. You can also substitute 6 ounces of semi-sweet chocolate chips for the squares of baking chocolate.

Ingredients

1 tablespoon instant espresso
⅓ cup boiling water
6 1-ounce squares semi-sweet baking
    chocolate, chopped
4 egg yolks
½ cup sugar
½ cup dry Marsala wine or dry sherry

2¾ cups whipping cream, divided
1 tablespoon instant coffee or espresso
1+ tablespoon granulated sugar
1 teaspoon cocoa powder
    shaved white or dark chocolate for
    garnish (optional)

Preparation

DISSOLVE 1 tablespoon instant espresso in the boiling water. Pour over chocolate pieces and stir until chocolate melts. You may have to put the mixture over low heat for a couple of minutes to completely melt the chocolate. When it is melted, set aside to cool slightly, until it is tepid.

USING a wooden spoon, mix egg yolks and ½ cup sugar together in a 2-quart saucepan, stirring until smooth. Add wine and stir until smooth. Place over low heat and cook until mixture thickens, stirring constantly, about 5 minutes. If making a double recipe, this will take 7 minutes. Mixture is thick enough when you can run your finger down the back of a spoon and leave a trail that doesn't fill in. Set pan in a bowl of ice and stir to cool quickly. If the egg mixture is not cooled completely, it will deflate the whipping cream when you fold it together.

IN A large mixing bowl, whip 2 cups of whipping cream on medium speed until stiff peaks form, about 1 minute. Gently fold cooled egg mixture into whipped cream. Gently fold espresso/chocolate mixture into the whipped cream until it is well incorporated. Spoon mousse into 8 6-ounce parfait glasses and chill in refrigerator at least 2 hours, or until firm.

TO SERVE, whip the remaining ¾ cup whipping cream into soft peaks with the instant coffee, sugar and cocoa powder. Place a scoop of whipping cream mixture on each parfait glass and top with shaved chocolate, if desired.

Serves 8

Bridge St., Helena, ca. 1869.

CULINARY SOURCES

CERTIFIED ORGANIC LAMB AND GRASS-FED BEEF AS WELL AS WOOL PRODUCTS

THIRTEEN MILE LAMB & WOOL COMPANY
13000 Springhill Road
Belgrade, MT 59714
406-388-4945 Fax 406-388-1956
www.lambandwool.com

SPECIALIZING IN WILD GAME & GOURMET PANTRY ITEMS

VALLEY GAME & GOURMET
P.O. Box 2713
Salt Lake City, UT 84110
www.valleygame.com
1-800-521-2156 or 801-521-2345

FRESH & SMOKED PHEASANTS, CHUKAR PARTRIDGE, QUAIL, DUCK, ALSO WILD RICE

OAKWOOD GAME FARMS
P.O. Box 274
Princeton, MN 55371
1-800-328-6647
www.oakwoodgamefarm.com

BUFFALO, ELK, VENSION, WILD BOAR, RABBIT, PHEASANT, QUAIL, DUCK, GOOSE; MUSHROOMS, BERRIES, AND FOIE GRAS

PRAIRIE HARVEST SPECIALTY FOODS
P.O. Box 1013
Spearfish, SD 57783
800-350-7166
www.prairieharvest.com

ANTELOPE, VENSION, WILD BOAR

BROKEN ARROW RANCH
P.O. Box 530
Ingram, TX 78025
1-800-962-4263
www.brokenarrowranch.com

TRUFFLES

THE TRUFFLE MARKET
P.O. Box 4234, Gettysburg, PA 17325
1-800-822-4003
www.trufflemarket.com

MUSHROOMS AND TRUFFLE OILS

GOURMET MUSHROOM PRODUCTS
P.O. Box 515 Graton, CA 9544
1-800-789-9121
www.gmushrooms.com

COMPLETE SELECTION OF CAVIAR - FOREIGN AND DOMESTIC

CAVIAR DIRECT
1-800-650-2828
www.caviar-direct.com
caviar@caviar-direct.com

COMPLETE SELECTION OF SPICES

PENZEYS SPICES
19300 West Janacek Court
P.O. Box 924
Brookfield, WI 53308
1-800-741-7787
www.penzeys.com

COMPLETE SELECTION OF GOURMET FOODS & GIFTS

IGOURMET
1-877-446-8763
www.igourmet.com

MONTANA-BASED GRASS-FED BISON, BEEF, LAMB & PORK; ALSO FREE-RANGE CHICKEN AND TURKEY; ORGANIC GRAINS & COFFEES

MONTANA COUNTRY MARKET – BELT, MT
1-877-342-4185
www.mtcountrymarket.com

ORGANIC MEATS AND PRODUCE

COMMUNITY FOOD CO-OP
908 W. Main Street
Bozeman, MT 59715
406-587-4039
www.bozo.coop

HUCKLEBERRY JAMS, SYRUPS, SAUCES

THE HUCKLEBERRY PEOPLE
1021 Waverly Street
Missoula, MT 59802
1-800-735-6462
www.huckleberrypeople.com

FAST DELIVERY FOR SPECIALTY FOODS (PREPARED CANNOLI SHELLS, PASTAS, ETC.) AND KITCHEN TOOLS

THE NEXT DAY GOURMET
www.nextdaygourmet.com

THE DEFINITIVE SOURCE FOR CULINARY QUESTIONS, DEFINITIONS AND RECIPES
www.epicurious.com

GLOSSARY

al dente	Used to describe pasta or other food that is cooked only until it offers a slight resistance when bitten into, but which is not overcooked.
aioli	A mayonnaise strongly seasoned with garlic or other seasoning, usually served as an accompaniment for fish, meats, and vegetables.
andouille	Spicy, heavily-smoked sausage.
bain-marie	A utensil used to gently cook sauces and soups so that they do not come to a boil. Similar to a double boiler if used on stovetop. In the oven, it can be a roasting pan filled with water in which the food container is placed.
béarnaise sauce	A classic French sauce made with vinegar, wine, tarragon, and shallots that have been reduced, finished with egg yolks and butter.
bake in hot water bath	See bain-marie above. In baking, you would put a shallow pan filled with a couple of inches of warm water in the oven and set your filled baking pan inside.
butterfly	To split food (such as shrimp or chicken breast) down the middle, but not completely through. The breast is opened to cook, resembling a butterfly.
capers	The flower bud of a bush native to the Mediterranean and parts of Asia. The small buds are picked, sun-dried, and then pickled in a vinegar brine.
chèvre cheese	French for "goat," chèvre is a pure white goat's-milk cheese with a tart flavor.
caul fat	The thin fat-laced membrane covering an animal's stomach.
chiffonade	A method similar to julienne, but refers mainly to cutting lettuce, endive, or herbs into thin, even strips.
chitterlings	Stomach lining (pork, beef, sheep).
chipotle	A dried, smoked, Jalepino. Has a sweet, almost chocolatey flavor.
chorizo	A spicy, coarsely ground pork sausage flavored with chile powder and garlic, usually in Mexican dishes.
clarified	Refers to a process of clearing a cloudy substance, such as in stocks or wines. Also refers to the process of melting unsalted butter until the foam rises. After skimming the foam off, the yellow liquid left can be heated to a much higher temperature than regular butter.
confectioners' sugar	Powdered sugar.
court bullion	A poaching liquid usually made up of vegetables, water, herbs and wine or vinegar.
crème anglaise	A cooked mixture of cream, sugar, egg yolks, and usually vanilla for flavoring. Often used as part of a dessert recipe.
crostini	Small, thin slices of toasted bread, usually brushed with olive oil. Means "little toasts" in Italian.
crème fraîche	A thick, velvety cream that can be boiled without curdling. Hard to find commercially and very expensive, but can be made simply by stirring well, 1 cup whipping cream and 2 tablespoons buttermilk in a glass container. Cover and let stand at room temperature (about 70°F) until thick (8-24 hours). Refrigerate up to 10 days.
de-bearding	To pull the threads towards the hinge of the mussel and tear out.

demi-glace	A rich brown sauce (usually meat stock) combined with Madiera or sherry and slowly cooked until it's reduced by half to a thick glaze.
deglaze	After food has been browned and fat removed, add a little wine or water to the skillet to loosen browned bits on the bottom to make a sauce.
demi-sec	In cooking, it refers to reducing by half. In wine, it refers to the level of sweetness.
dore	Golden brown.
foie gras	The term generally used for goose liver.
frenched	To trim fat or bone from a cut of meat.
gazpacho	A cold, summertime vegetable soup.
gratinée	To brown (usually crumbs and butter) under a broiler or with a torch.
gremulata	A garnish made of minced parsley, lemon peel, and garlic to add a fresh, sprightly flavor.
gumbo filé	Powdered, dried leaves of the sassafras tree, generally used in Creole cooking.
julienne	A method of cutting vegetables into thin strips, usually about 1 inch by $\frac{1}{16}$ inch.
kosher salt	An additive-free coarse-grained salt used in the preparation of meat by gourmet cooks who prefer its texture and flavor.
mascarpone	An Italian cream cheese; double- to triple-rich and buttery.
meunière	Lightly dusting a meat or fish in flour and sauteeing in butter, usually with lemon juice sprinkled on top.
morel mushroom	An edible wild mushroom belonging to the same fungus species as the truffle.
mirin	A sweet, rice wine used in cooking to sweeten meat or fish dishes.
napoleon	A dish made with a variety of layers, usually a dessert.
nappe	Usually referring to a coating, such as a sauce that has thickened enough to coat a spoon.
Oban wafers	A type of chocolate wafer. (See Culinary Sources.)
paella	A Spanish rice dish with a variety of meats or shellfish, or vegetables (garlic, onions, peas, artichoke hearts, and tomatoes) usually flavored with saffron.
pancetta	A slightly salty Italian bacon cured with salt and spices, but not smoked.
Panko	Coarse bread crumbs (Japanese) used for coating fried foods. Create a deliciously crunchy outer crust. Available in supermarkets.
prosciutto	Italian word for ham; seasoned, salt-cured and air-dried, but not smoked.
purée	To grind or mash food until it's completely smooth, by using a food processor, a blender, or by forcing the food through a sieve.
ragout	A stew made of meats or vegetables, well-seasoned and thickened.
ramekin	An individual earthenware baking dish (3 to 4 inches in diameter) that resembles a miniature soufflé dish.

reduce (reduction)	To boil a liquid rapidly (stock, wine, or a sauce mixture) until the volume reduces by evaporation, thickening the consistency and intensifying the flavor.
render	To convert or melt down fat by slow heating.
ribbon stage	The stage in a recipe when the ingredients you are beating (usually egg yolks and sugar) thicken enough to flow from your whisk or spoon in a continuous ribbon.
roux	A mixture of equal parts flour and butter used to thicken sauces. Cooking different lengths of time results in different flavors and colors.
sauté	To quickly cook food over direct heat in a small amount of hot oil.
shallot	Member of the onion family.
steep	To soak dry ingredients (leaves, coffee, herbs, spices, etc.) in liquid (usually hot) until the flavor is infused into the liquid.
sushi rice	A round-grained rice that becomes slightly sticky when cooked, so that it can be mixed with other ingredients and shaped in a roll.
sweat	To cook vegetables slowly in their own juices. A little butter or oil is often used to start the process, and then the mixture is covered to let the moisture in the vegetables release.
tapenade	A spread or condiment, usually consisting of capers, olives, anchovies mashed with olive oil.
tartare	Often refers to a raw meat dish.
tartar sauce	A sauce usually served with fish, and consisting of mayonnaise, capers, onion, olives and pickles.
temper	Most often refers to slightly warming beaten eggs, by rapidly stirring a little of the hot ingredients into them, before adding them to the hot mixture so that they will combine without solidifying.
tomato stricia	Commercially-available tomatoes cut in strips and packed in a puree.
Tobikko	Caviar, flying fish roe.
tripe	Most commonly, the lining of the beef stomach, although it could be pork or sheep. Usually fairly tough and requires longer cooking periods.
truffle	A fungus that is cultivated primarily in France and Italy today. It is grown underneath the ground, usually at the base of certain trees such as oak and chestnut. Highly prized for its earthy, aromatic nature.
truffle oil	Truffle oil is created when truffles are soaked in olive oil.
tuile	A flavored thin, crisp cookie that is usually curved.
U-15 shrimp	Pertains to the size of the shrimp; the number following the U denotes the number of shrimp per pound (approximately).
wilted spinach /lettuce	Using a steam process to wilt spinach or lettuce, or drizzling a hot liquid or bacon grease over the vegetables to cause them to wilt.
zest	The brightly colored outermost skin layer of citrus fruit, removed with a zester, grater, or knife.

ABOUT THE PUBLISHERS

Chuck and Blanche started Wilderness Adventures Press, Inc. in 1993, publishing outdoor and sporting books. Along with hunting and fishing, they love fine dining, good wines, and traveling. They have always been able to "sniff out" the most outstanding and interesting restaurants in any city they visit.

On weekends, they experiment in the kitchen, cooking a variety of fish and meats, as well as preparing the harvest from their time in the field. This love of cooking has resulted in a large library of cookbooks, and has inspired them to create a series of cookbooks based on their love of travel and fine dining.

Chuck and Blanche make their home in Gallatin Gateway, Montana, along with their four German wirehaired pointers.

Photo Copyrights/Credits

Front cover, left to right: ©La Provence; ©Fly Fishers Inn; ©The Granary; ©Triple Creek Ranch; ©Chico Hot Springs; ©Montana Historical Society; ©Montana Historical Society; ©Triple Creek Ranch; ©John Bozeman's Bistro; ©Chico Hot Springs; ©Montana Historical Society; ©Corner House Grill; **Back cover, left to right:** ©Big Hole Lodge; ©The Granary; ©Triple Creek Ranch; ©Triple Creek Ranch; ©Corner House Grill; ©Chico Hot Springs

i: ©Montana Historical Society; **iii, iv:** ©Blanche T. Johnson; **v:** ©Montana Historical Society; **vi, vii:** ©Blanche T. Johnson; **viii, xii:** ©Montana Historical Society; **1, 2, 5:** ©Enzo Mediterranean Bistro; **7:** ©Q Cuisine **12:** ©Blanche T. Johnson; **13, 14:** ©The Granary; **19, 20, 21, 24, 25:** © Walkers Grill; **27, 28-top, 30:** ©Chico Hot Springs; **28-bottom:** Gallayin County Historical Society; **35,36:** ©Adagio; **42:** ©Montana Historical Society; **43-45:** ©Second Street Bistro; **50:** ©Montana Historical Society; **51:** ©Blanche T. Johnson; **52:** ©Boodles; **55, 57-59, 63:** ©Blanche T. Johnson; **65, 66, 69:** ©Gallatin River Lodge; **70:** ©Montana Historical Society; **71-74:** ©John Bozeman's Bistro; **76:** ©Gallatin County Historical Society; **77, 78, 79-left, 80:** ©320 Guest Ranch; **79-right:** ©Gallatin County Historical Society; **82:** ©Montana Historical Society; **83-85:** Buck's T-4 Lodge; **89-91, 93:** ©Lone Mountain Ranch; **95-96:** ©The Timbers at Moonlight Basin; **100:** ©Continental Divide; **103-105:** ©Potosi Hot Springs; **109-111:** ©Big Hole Lodge; **116:** ©Montana Historical Society; **117-118:** ©Jackson Hot Springs Lodge; **125-126, 129, 131:** ©Big Hole Crossing; **133-135, 137, 141:** ©Triple Creek Ranch; **143-144, 146, 148:** ©Red Bird; **149-152:** ©Double Arrow Resort; **153, 154-bottom, 155-bottom:** ©La Provence; **154-top, 155-top:** ©Ted Habarth; **156:** ©Montana Historical Society; **161-162:** ©Cafe Max; **166, 167, 168-bottom:** ©Michael Hewston; **168-top, 169:** ©Kalispell Grand Hotel; **175-176:** ©Corner House Grill; **181:** ©Montana Historical Society; **183:** ©Montana Historical Society; **187:** ©Art Today; **188, 192:** ©Pollo Grill; **193-194:** ©Tupelo Grille; **198:** ©Montana Historical Society; **199-201, 203:** ©St. Mary Lodge; **209:** ©Donnie Sexton/Travel Montana; **210:** ©Montana Historical Society; **213-215:** ©Grand Union Hotel; **217:** ©Union Grill; **218:** ©Montana Historical Society; **219:** ©Donnie Sexton/Travel Montana; **220:** ©Jen Tzenis; **224:** ©Montana Historical Society; **225-226, 228-229:** ©Fly Fishers Inn; **232:** ©Montana Historical Society

INDEX